Walking in Olde Wickford

The History of Quality Hill & Talbot's Corner

One House at a Time

2012

G. Timothy Cranston

Other books by G. Timothy Cranston:

Walking in Olde Wickford:
The History of Elamsville & the Wickford Business District
One Building at a Time - 2011

Walking in Olde Wickford:
The History of Old Wickford One House at a Time - 2010

Images of America: North Kingstown 1880-1920 - 2005

DEDICATION

The ties that have bound the community of Wickford
together across the countless generations that have gone
on before are all rooted in family. I can think of no two
people who better personify the critical importance that
family plays in a place like this, and I thank them for
reaching out and including me in their greater family.
Tom and Erma Peirce, this one's for you.

CONTENTS

FOREWORD

*C*ontinuing on with the same theme from Volume 1, where we looked at Micheal de Guzman's memories of growing up in Wickford during the 1940's, and Volume 2 where I reminisced about a 1960's childhood in the village, this volume will begin with the late Walter Hazard Sr.'s recollection of a boyhood in Wickford during the 1920's. Walter Hazard grew up to be a remarkable gentleman, a surveyor, draftsman, and construction engineer who was admired and respected by all he came in contact with; to local Swamp Yankees and other staunch South County-ites all of whom were fiercely Republican, he only had one character flaw, and that was his insistence on belonging to the Democratic Party. Even in this though, Walter Hazard's dogged determination was admired. Between 1938 and 1974, Hazard ran for elective office every time, including a number of campaigns against my grandfather George C. Cranston, winning only once in 1950. Later in his life, as the pendulum swung back towards the political party of his choice, Walter Hazard did serve three terms as a Rhode Island State Senator. Walter Hazard originally wrote this wonderful piece as a part of North Kingstown's Tricentennial Celebration in 1974. It is reprinted here with the permission of my friend Walter Hazard Jr.

An ancient village is the way that I would describe my first impression of the small town of Wickford in the late fall of 1918. My mother, myself and my two brothers had just moved from Providence. World War I was in progress. People felt the hardship of many shortages. Sugar and meat were scarce, as well as money. We also had personal difficulties. My seafaring father's separation from the family made my mother the breadwinner with no income at all.

We moved into a two tenement house on Main Street next to what used to be the Standard office. Viewed through my seven-year-old eyes, it was an old grey weather-beaten place, reminding me of a cold-water flat. We moved to Wickford because my younger brother was suffering from a spinal disorder. The doctor had advised us to get him out in the sun. Wickford was right on the water, located on a beautiful cove which flowed into the clear Narragansett Bay. Its invigoration climate, with its salt water, pure air and gentle breezes, would cure him. However, he would be restricted to a frame for two years and then into a cast for another eighteen months. My mother devoted her life to restoring his health and making him as robust as he could be.

The community was right there pitching in. There was dedication and friendly assistance among the people. I recall we needed a boat. Allie Saunders, as some natives will remember, ran the boat yard across the cove and supplied the boat and oars. Someone else furnished a wagon that the frame could be laid in, so my mother could cart him around. Soon his body was tan and healthy, his sunburned face aglow.

Time passed quickly. Going to grammar school and doing some gardening in the small yard kept us busy. In addition to her chores, my mother had regular dealings with the Wickford Savings Bank. She developed a friendly relationship with Joseph G. Reynolds, the manager and vice-president of the bank, who owned one of the first cars in town, the Dixie Flyer. About two years later, they married. We moved to his house on Pleasant Street, which was one of the loveliest homes in Wickford (it is now owned by Mrs. A. J. Himes).

I remember this house with great joy. It was quite a change from the one we had originally moved into. Our new home was a white stately house with Colonial charm. It had a number of spacious rooms, high ceilings, and two cozy fireplaces. In the large yard were a cherry and pear tree. However, there were drawbacks. To take a bath and keep your water supply, it was necessary to use a hand pump. The water journeyed from attic to tub. The same water was used during the week coming down through the pipes. Therefore, we didn't go looking for too many baths. Can you blame us? Also, because of the cost, eggs were in short supply during the winter. Therefore, the procedure would be to get the eggs in late fall, put them into a brine and store them away in your cellar. So with your precious eggs safely tucked away, you would feel a certain sense of security knowing you could cook one anytime you wanted to.

The kitchen stove we had was one of the old coal-burning or wood-burning ones. The wood was brought from the farmers and stored in the cellars. Although it was difficult to maintain the temperature of the stove, I still recall mince pies, and all the tasty foods that were cooked on it. Another not-too-luxurious feature of the house was the three-holer out in the yard. The paper that we used was from the wrappings of an orange. But despite the few luxuries, we were grateful to have such a beautiful and did our best to maintain it. My mother felt it was our duty. So we cleaned it spotlessly every Friday or Saturday. After that was done, we went out in the town, running errands, mowing lawns or cleaning other houses.

Since we had no allowances in those days, we depended on the work done in the community for our spending money. We used that for the pleasure to sit excitedly in the dark theater at the Odd Fellows Hall, now the Wickford Auction Theater, on Saturday night and watch the silent movies. Miller's Hall, located down in back of the present Earnshaw's, was another movie house open during the week. King Gorman, who hailed from East Greenwich, was the movie magnate. He would haul the films back and forth. We'd get the first reel or the first act. Then he'd dash that back to East Greenwich. Among the two or three houses, we all saw the same movie on that one night. For me, this was the only recreation in the town between 1918-1925.

But for others, there were different activities. Take Brown Street, for example, which was the business part of Wickford and still is. Next to the bridge, opposite Ryan's Market, was the pool room and bowling alleys run by Mr. Spink. A lot of kids made it a gathering place. But my mother felt those were strictly taboo places to go. So we never did learn those games. Besides going regularly to the movies, there also was the North Kingstown Library to frequent for the early part of the evening. The two librarians, Annie and Elizabeth Merithew, were always very kind. When I'd be browsing around for the latest detective stories and Rover Boy books, they promptly and properly came to my rescue. Dignified and respected, they were an integral part of the town.

Also, much of our time was spent in the church. It was an important aspect of community life. There were three churches: the Baptist, the Catholic, and the

Episcopal. Very little socializing went on among the three groups. Originally when we moved to Wickford we attended the Episcopal Church, because it was nearer to my mother's childhood faith. We always enjoyed going, especially at Christmas time, when we got some small gift such as a toy, cookies, or candies. After my mother's marriage to Mr. Reynolds, we joined the Baptist Church. We were allowed to go out on Thursday nights if we went to prayer meetings. So naturally we went. The best part of the service was the fervent Amens that went with the praying. In my naïve youth, I thought the word was a signal that meant shut up. On Sunday all the families went to church. A plate would be passed and we would take communion. I will always remember Hattie Reynolds who played the organ. She sat up in front with a great big mirror facing her, so she could tell who was there and where everybody was seated. That was how she knew when to start the music. That ritual in the service remains a treasured memory for me.

In addition to the weekly services, I clearly recall the Baptist Church's special events. I especially enjoyed the Evangelists coming to town. They would rouse up the population and increase the membership of the church. One charismatic Evangelist was like Billy Graham. In those days, he was comparable to Billy Sunday. He'd be there all week, doing his best for religion. Some people would stand up one night and some another. Finally, on the third night with many others I stood up and gave myself to Christ. Weeks later we were baptized in the bathtub on the stage of the Quidnessett Baptist Church in the dead of winter. In the hot summer, the procedure was to be bathed in the beach at the end of Main Street. You were completely dunked in a black robe.

Along with church-going, school was another essential part of my growing up. The teachers I had were welcome additions to the North Kingstown School System. I had Edward Pratt, now a former principal of the high school, in the 7th and 8th grades. He was a handsome, suave man who still hasn't lost those qualities today. Hiram A. Davis (former school superintendent) now retired was my teacher in high school when he came to North Kingstown as the principal. There weren't many school activities to participate in. Although there were track meets, there was no way to get to them, unless you wanted to walk and that usually was for miles and miles. The only real excitement we had was the Chautauga traveling road show that came from Pennsylvania. On the days that it was in Wickford, we were let out early from school to see it. I recall it fondly because it was one of the few pleasures I was afforded in my childhood. Work took up a lot of my free time.

I had a job at Ryan's Market which is a landmark in Wickford. It was run by Edward Ryan originally. (By the way, he was a good friend of Captain Frank Smith who worked for Fleischman's Yeast. Between them they were quite successful in the stock market.) My Saturday pay at Ryan's netted me the grand sum of two dollars for the entire day! I enjoyed my work and especially being around Mr. Ryan, who was a fine person, raised a wonderful family. He died a few years ago, but Mrs. Ryan is still with us. I also sold newspapers from Sealey's Ice-Cream Parlor. They were delivered for 14 cents a week for six days. We made 2 cents from each buyer, and if we had a good customer, we'd get a 5 cent tip. If you made two dollars a week, why, that was fabulous! Mowing lawns was another way of earning extra money. My territory consisted of the elegant lawns on Main Street and on West Main Street, too. Among my employers were Thaddeus Hunt, the manager of the Industrial Bank, and Tom Lewis who was one of the legendary fishing Lewis Brothers. He went fishing religiously each morning in his boat at daybreak. I also cleaned the lawns of Mr. Ward and Peter Byrnes who ran the original greenhouse on West Main Street. There were times when I worked in the greenhouse and in the gardens. In addition, I worked for Abby Gardner who lived off Main Street and for Joe Green who owned the mills in Hamilton and was considered a power in the town.

We also had an eccentric gentleman in the town named Dubbey Grandison, who lived in an old desolate boat down in Wickford Cove. He had what they called a honey cart. While I was mowing lawns, he would go through town on a horse and clean out the cesspools. While I don't know where he dumped the stuff, somehow he got rid of it. Later on, with my earnings from my odd jobs, I bought a Model T Ford Suburban from Louis Ward. I cut the top off, put two or three barrels in it and decided to try what Dubbey was doing. So I began to go around cleaning cesspools myself for some additional money. When recalling my growing up in Wickford, it seemed that school, church, and work dominated my existence. But I did manage to find time to just go around talking to the local people. Everybody knew each other on a one-to-one basis. So the intimacy and colorful charm of the townspeople and its quaint places will always remain close to my heart.

I remember William P. Hambly. Besides being a tax collector and the coroner, he was the town barber, with a shop on Brown Street, next to what is now Ryan's Liquor Store. He used to cut hair for the mere price of 25 cents. He had false teeth which he chewed on all the time. Unfortunately, they really smelled bad. What an ordeal we went through, just sitting on that barber chair. The unpleasant odors were enough to choke us to death and make us regret spending the 25 cents. It was sad that mouthwash hadn't been invented at that time.

Next to his store was Dr. Young, a white-bearded pharmacist who really looked the part. He was a calm and very dignified man who lived on Pleasant Street, near the water. We bought our penny candy in his store. It was also hard to resist his double-scooped ice-cream cones which were only a nickel.

Next to Dr. Young's was the Wickford Club. In those days, it consisted of all the political henchmen in the local area. They had a German-born manager who knew how to make brew. I used to deliver newspapers there and the horrible smells of the home brew were enough to make me race down those stairs. Finally, I got used to it. I just chalked it up as another part of all the goings-on on Brown Street in Wickford. Going south on Brown Street was the local barbershop. Next to it, located on the main street where Earnshaw's Drugstore is now, was a small house. At the time, I had no idea that it was a speakeasy but it flourished for many years. Coming farther down on Brown Street, near today's Hospital Trust Bank, was a grain depot and a shop run by Mr. Dixon, an elder in the Baptist Church. At church, he played the oboe which gave off huge grunts, while the organ played. He was quite an interesting man but what fascinated me most about him was that he had the first electric car run by batteries. He even had a place to charge the batteries in his establishment. That ornate glass enclosed car astonished my 10-year-old eyes for it was one of the few electric cars on the market at that time.

Another unforgettable member of the community was our former resident doctor, Dr. Metcalf, who lived on Hamilton Avenue. He was completely dedicated to his profession. Originally with a horse and wagon and then later with a car, he never failed to make a house call. I'm sure in many cases he never got paid. His work mattered to him more than any monetary reward. Furthermore, he specialized in everything, and probably had as much knowledge as any medical man today. After Dr. Metcalf or concurrently with him was Dr. Manning. He was our chief physician for many, many years. These gentlemen were highly respected and depended upon by the community for their medical needs.

As far as legal order was concerned, we had a hard-working Town Clerk named John B. Peirce, who carefully kept all the town records. Mr. Peirce had information on just about anything one needed to know. Maintaining the law was the job of the police department. In the early days, it consisted of one sole man named Thomas Peirce. He was our first chief of police, and lived on West Main Street, opposite the funeral parlor. He had no vehicle whatsoever to get around and I remember one night someone broke into a house across the street from us. By simply walking over, Chief Peirce manacled the culprit, marched him over to the jail in the bottom of the town hall and locked him up. That was that! Later on, Scott Edwards was our chief of police. He operated out of what is now Dutchland Farms and with a one-man force. About that time, the State Police moved in and were located opposite Barber's Hardware on Brown Street. This became the headquarters of the original State Police Barracks when the force was organized in 1929 by Colonel Chafee. Wickford accepted the State Police with much friendliness. There were good feelings on both sides. Unfortunately, a tragic event occurred. One of the original commanders of the barracks was killed by a derelict up on Prospect Street when he went to rouse him out of a barn. This incident resulted in a lot of sorrow and sympathy among the people.

In terms of the political picture, the town was run by Colonel Robert Rodman, one of the brothers who owned the Rodman Mills. (In the late 1920's there were some stories going around, and, if they are to be believed, the elections were pretty much controlled by the Republicans.) However, Colonel Rodman ran the town efficiently for those days. He was a generous and kind man. Mrs. Rodman, a very lovely woman, devoted a great deal of her time at what is now the Ladd School for the Retarded.

So, all in all, everybody in a position of service was dedicated. Wickford was a neighborly, quiet place to dwell in. However, even in the most small, peaceful towns, there is bound to be some flurry. Such was the case here during Prohibition. Roman's Vineyards were located what is now Quonset Naval Air Base. Mrs. Romano, the boss, was a very strong-willed woman. A number of her sons grew up to become successful in politics. Anyway, all the politicians knew where Romano's Vineyards were. In fact, they could get there blindfolded, as that was where they could buy anisette or liquor illegally.

Rum Runners were also quite plentiful in the day and inside the 12-mile limit. One of the big locations was down at South Ferry. I can't recall all the speedboats that used to get in, but one of them used to dock in there underneath one of the homes. Some boats would be moored in Wickford and in East Greenwich. If it was a foggy night, they probably had a better chance of getting in. Once in awhile they would get caught. Things would get rough and there would be some shooting out in the bay. But despite the danger it went on anyway. I always remember one man telling my stepfather that one more load and he would have made a million dollars on running rum. However, this golden dream was shattered when the Internal Revenue Agents stepped in and grabbed all the liquor. Sadly, he went back to the restaurant business. But evidently he put a lot of money aside anyway. So, with the exception of the hustle and bustle of Prohibition, the small town of Wickford ran its day-to-day course quietly. The towns-people went about their leisurely business and pastimes. A favorite pleasure of mine was being near the sea. It relaxed me and gave me a feeling of exhilaration. And seeing those boats come in, why, that was pure ecstasy!

I'll always remember the New England Steamship Company that ran all the palatial sound steamers from New Bedford, Fall River, Newport, Providence, and New London. Many of us were connected with them in some way. My father was Captain of the New England Steamship Lines. My grandfather had the distinctive title before him. So the sea really flowed and throbbed through my blood. The father of Halfdan Anderson, who lives in town now, was captain of the *General*, which stopped in Wickford. Wealthy people from New York used to come down on Friday to Wickford Junction. They would get off the train, and then go right to the dock at Wickford. They would board the *General* to go to Newport, and then grandly exit to their majestic homes. Captain Anderson served them well for many, many years.

The local train from Wickford to Wickford Junction was also an attraction. Carl Pratt, our local man at that time, was a fireman on the train. After the train was disbanded, we had a bus from Wickford. The railroad station in Wickford, is still in existence, but is used as a power equipment shop. At right angles to the railroad were the trolley tracks of the Seaview Railroad which ran from Providence to Wakefield.

Wickford was considered in those days a summer resort for people who weren't of the Newport breed, but probably were what we all the middle class today. They would stay in the Wickford House or the Cold Spring House in the summer. Mother Prentice ran the Wickford House at that time. She was sort of a stern, but friendly woman whose scrumptious food was known throughout the state. Johnnycakes were one of her specialties. So Wickford became a summer resort and flourished in this respect. We who were natives, who spent our time mowing lawns barefooted all summer, didn't mix too much with the summer crowd. We were pretty much on our own. There were things to do, and we had a few pleasures. But first, some historical background on one of the 'grand escapades.'

At that time when the boats were running to Newport, the Rodman, Lafayette and Shady Lea Mills and the boat to Newport all used soft coal. At the foot of

Main Street, the dock was covered with huge piles of soft coal which was transported by truck to Lafayette and other locations. Over at the boat dock were more huge piles of soft coal that were used for the steamer *General*. Huge lifts existed in all the coal yards. The more daring youths would climb to the top and dive into the coal. I have to admit that I wasn't one of the more courageous. I was too chicken, so I would just enjoy watching the others but this one was on my summer highlights.

Another pastime was gathering fish on the beach. Here, I was an active participant. Shellfish were quite abundant, as were the native scallops which we used to pick up on the beach at Wickford. We'd eat them raw and they tasted terrific! Once, I got into a private bed of quahogs that belong to Joseph Smith. (It seemed amusing to me at that time, but Mr. Smith failed to see the humor.) Oysters were harvested by two or three companies off of what is now Quonset and Shore Acres. There were two large oyster houses at the foot of Pleasant Street and Saturday night, it was usually a family ritual to go down and get a peck of oysters in the shell, bring them home, open them up in a hurry and eat them, savoring each bite.

In the late 20's things were beginning to jump. The big name bands would come to Narragansett to Johnny Miller's and we'd all rush down to be there on a Saturday night. In those days, the price of admission was a dollar a piece but we'd get to hear the swinging sounds of Olson, Benny Goodman, and many others. Gradually activities began to move faster than they had over the previous years. Sound movies were coming into being, and radio, which started with the original crystal set, became widespread.

During World Series time schools were let out a little early. We all eagerly formed down on Brown Street by the park where Joe Sealey and Roger Rodman had a big blackboard. Two or three people would anxiously listen with their earphones to the radio and highlights of the World Series games would be posted on this blackboard as they were received. As scores were written down, we'd all cheer, hoot, whistle, or stomp.

Another exciting event that happened during the late 1920's was the historic flight of Lindbergh. After he had flown his solo to Europe, he came back and toured some of the cities including Providence. He landed at what is now Quonset Point and was grandly escorted to Providence in a large, open touring car. Most of the people had to walk to see him, and joyously we all did, all the way to Camp Avenue. After a parade and a reception, amidst lots of applause, cheers, and good wishes, he flew off again. My own heart was bursting with pride and happiness. I marked this down as a welcome addition to the momentous occasions that happened during my high school years.

I must admit that the last year of high school was probably one of the most joyous for me. The school was small and everybody knew one another on a personal basis since there were just 24 in the graduating class. In a senior play, "Mrs. Tempe's Telegram," I made my acting debut. We also had an expanded athletic program and Mr. Pratt was coach of the first football team in 1929. There were sixteen people on it—everyone played—and there were no rest periods during a game. That year North Kingstown beat South Kingstown for the first time

WALTER ROBINSON HAZARD
"Keed"-"Walt"

Walt is the "guy" of the happy grin and flashing black eyes which give life to his lazy appearance. We always know when 'Walt" is bored for he begins to chew paper and starts an under-toned conversation. They say that he is one reason why girls leave home. Well, what girl wouldn't be interested in a four letter man. Go to it, "Keed," you're doing fine; keep it up in Boston with Paul.

1929 North Kingstown Yearbook page with Walter Hazard.

in many years in four different sports. And I must mention here, that there was a girl's basketball team as well. (We were really head of Women's Lib.) Then it was over–the 1929 graduation came. Our class motto was "Life is what we make it," but it was the year of the Depression. It was a time of much despair. Money was scarce. Jobs were few. To go on to college was rare. There was no funding of state or federal education. I went to Wentworth Institute in Boston to study architectural construction, but for only a short time, because of lack of funds. I then went to work on a steamship. From there on, it was a matter of taking various menial jobs just to survive. Finally in 1930, I became a surveyor's aid for the State of Rhode Island for $19 a week. I was lucky. Men were selling apples for a nickel on the street. The towns-people's faces showed the economic hardship and hopelessness that we were going through.

As I look at prosperous Wickford today, it is hard to believe that we lived through such a time. In a nostalgic sense, I gaze at this completely modernized New England town, population of 25,000 with all the hustle and bustle of contemporary life. It is amazing to recollect that Wickford started from such humble beginnings. When I was growing up, it had only 4,000 inhabitants, simple community services, a leisurely atmosphere, and an old-fashioned closeness between the townspeople. But that was all then. One can never get back those people, places and events. For it all happened once upon a time.

ACKNOWLEDGEMENTS

There have been so many people who have helped me along the way as I researched and wrote this book. I'm sure I'll forget someone and for that I apologize in advance; here are the folks whose contributions were such that their names stuck in the great colander that is my memory.

Local Wickford-ites, past and present, were invaluable in their recollections of the way things were and the many photographs, notebooks, diaries, and scrapbooks that they allowed me access to. These folks include Thomas, Erma, & Rachel Peirce, the lovely KarenLu LaPolice, Jean Chapman, Harry & Joe Beckwith, Grace Moran, Gladys Bailey, Albert Emery, Peter Ward, Winston Stadig Jr., Walter Hazard Jr., Penny (Aldrich) Geuss, Gail (Cranston) Seymour, Harry & Jan Lewis, Win & Kathy Brown, Olga Caluori Wilcox & Rachel Wilcox Christiansen, and Roger & Gordon Walsh. Thanks to all of you for trusting me with your memories and your artifacts from the past.

A handful of scholarly folks were also invaluable as both sources and sounding boards during the process. Among these are Rick Greenwoood and Jeff Emidy at RI Historic Preservation, kindred spirit, URI professor and "train nut" Frank Heppner, David Brussat and Paul Davis at the Providence Journal, the helpful folks at the URI Library Special Collections Dept., the good people at the Nantucket Historical Society, my good friend George Zachorne, and Steve Tyson Jr. of the Architectural Preservation Group. A special tip of the hat goes out to RI State Archivist Kenneth Carlson who could seemingly answer any question and my friend Neil Dunay. I'm a paranoid soul by nature and I double check every bit of information I'm given for accuracy; after a while though, I just trusted what Neil and Ken passed on to me. They are just that good at what they do.

Once again, a "thank you kindly" must be extended to Neil Dunay and Darrell McIntire. These two busy gentlemen were gracious enough to take the time to proofread and edit this work, an invaluable contribution.

And, like a broken record, I have got to say once again, what would I have done without the skills, patience, perseverance, and friendship of Rachel Peirce? This book is as much hers as it is mine. She, like her father Tom, truly understands how special this little village is. We share a connection to Wickford that extends back to its very beginnings. Rachel gets it and I hope after you read this book, you'll get it too. Thank you Rachel.

INTRODUCTION

This section of the village of Wickford is truly near and dear to my heart. It was not only my home for the first nine years of my life, I lived first at 154 West Main Street and then at 140 West Main Street, but it, as the location of my maternal grandparents home, was my one true constant as I grew up. No matter what type of turmoil our lives existed within, my sisters, brother and I could always count on the constancy and dependability of Grandpa and Grandma St. Pierre and their wonderful home at 159 West Main Street. Our whole world could have descended into chaos and disarray up on Annaquatucket Road, the place we settled after leaving Wickford proper, but everything would just feel all right again as soon as we set foot on the piazza (that's what they called the front porch) or sat ourselves down on the divan (which was called a couch or sofa nearly everywhere else in the entire universe). Grandpa and Grandma were truly creatures of habit back then. The only bread they ate was white bread from the Cushman's Bakery truck or Arnolds Bread from the market, on which they always spread fancy Dundee marmalade that came in a ceramic jar. Their meat, all their food for that matter, always came from Ryan's Market, grandpa always bought a Chevy, and they loved their family, friends, and neighbors without ceasing. Yes, they were creatures of habit, but nearly every habit was good and right and steady as the Rock of Gibraltar. On top of all this, my father's siblings all lived here on West Main Street. This made it a place full of aunts and uncles and cousins as well. Family friends resided here too; memories of all of them, John Ward and his humor and stories, Mrs. Metz and Mrs. Ross and their maternal kindnesses,

the Crooker clan, the Moffitt family, brave and kind Dr. Kuzma who spirited his family out of Eastern Europe just as the Iron Curtain began to fall; all of the memories surrounding all of these relatives and friends wander back to me each and every time I walk up or down the sidewalks of Quality Hill. Join me while I journey back there.

Four generations on the St. Pierre divan: Jean (St. Pierre) Cranston, Paul St. Pierre and Caroline St. Pierre holding Tim Cranston.

The History of the "Quality Hill"

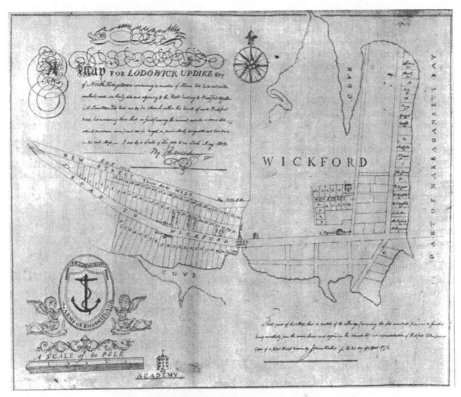

**A Map for Lodowick Updike Esq. of North Kingstown
done by Caleb Harris in 1802.**

In early 1802, 77 year old Lodowick Updike II, son of Daniel Updike, surveyed and platted out his real estate holdings on either side of the "Grand Highway," the road leading from the Boston Post Road into the village of Wickford, for sale as individual house lots. In doing this, he continued the business strategy begun by his grandfather Lodowick I in 1709, when he first developed the planned community of Updike's Newtown, later named Wickford, as well as the later development of the adjacent Elamsville plat in 1795 by the three daughters of Samuel Boone Jr. That Elamsville land had been purchased from Daniel Updike by Samuel Boone Sr. in 1727.

As a part of this process, Lodowick II hired surveyor Caleb Harris to survey out 76 house lots in this area and an additional 14 house lots adjacent to the recently relocated Old Narragansett Church on Church Lane in Wickford proper. In general, each of the 90 house lots identified possessed "3 rods" of frontage on a street. Harris also did the survey work to lay out a new road which ran roughly parallel and north of the existing Grand Highway and served as the frontage for a number of these lots. He utilized a previous Wickford land survey done in April 1773 by local surveyor John Northup as his starting point for this work. He delivered his final product, titled "A Map for Lodowick Updike Esq. of North Kingstown" to Updike in May of 1802. Due to the unpopularity of the northern lots with their frontage on what was essentially a street on paper only, they did not sell, and subsequently Updike's "New Street – three rods wide" was never actually constructed and those 24 lots were merged with lots directly to their south. The street plan did however serve as the basis for a private road utilized by Oliver Spink, then Daniel Lawton and finally George Merithew as the farm access road between the main farm complex at the old Samuel Brenton house at the road's intersection with Brown/Bridge Street and the large farm fields at what is now Wilson Park.

Although this new real estate development was surrounded to the north by land still owned largely by the Updike clan, the land to the west and south of the Harris platted lots was owned by the inter-related Boone-Spink-Franklin family and included a number of homes that predated the 1802 survey, but do not show up on the May 1802 Harris map as they were not Updike owned. Indeed, the intersection of the Boston Post Road and the Grand Highway was originally known as Franklin's Corner, named after John and Hannah (Boone) Franklin who ran an inn there. In later years, when that same inn was owned by the Talbot family of Providence, the location became known as Talbot's Corner. Harris did make note of the extant Bissell and Holley houses which were demolished in the early 1800s, the Old Narragansett Church, the Washington Academy, the Samuel Brenton house, at that time owned by Oliver Spink, as well as Lodowick's own

The Samuel Brenton house, owned by Oliver Spink.

Lodowick Updike's house which was demolished in 1948.

house; which was demolished in June of 1948 and replaced by the St. Paul's Parish House.

Although a brisk business in speculative land purchases followed the 1802 platting of the area, largely by members of the Holloway family and individuals in some way related to the Updikes, very little actual construction occurred in those first years. When Lodowick Updike II died in June of 1804, the remaining unsold lots were left in his will to his children who continued marketing and selling them in the same fashion. As an unintended consequence of the devastating hurricane, "The Great Gale of 1815," local folks began calling Lodowick's development Quality Hill with the critically important "quality" being its location on higher ground beyond the reaches of the destructive storm surge of this well-remembered weather event. The name stuck, and development on this high ground moved forward at a quicker pace following the storm.

The civically-minded Updike family, which had previously donated the land upon which the Old Narragansett Church was relocated to, in 1806, through the generosity of Daniel and James Updike, donated another parcel of land to the community for the construction of the North Kingstown Town House. The Town House is not only the first government building in the town; it is also one of oldest extant local town meeting halls in southern Rhode Island.

To quote my predecessor in local history Hunter C. White, "Unlike other sections of Wickford this was a purely residential section and it has always remained so." This does not, however, indicate that the stories that spring from these numerous old homes are not interesting and exciting. Quality Hill was, and still is, a wonderful place.

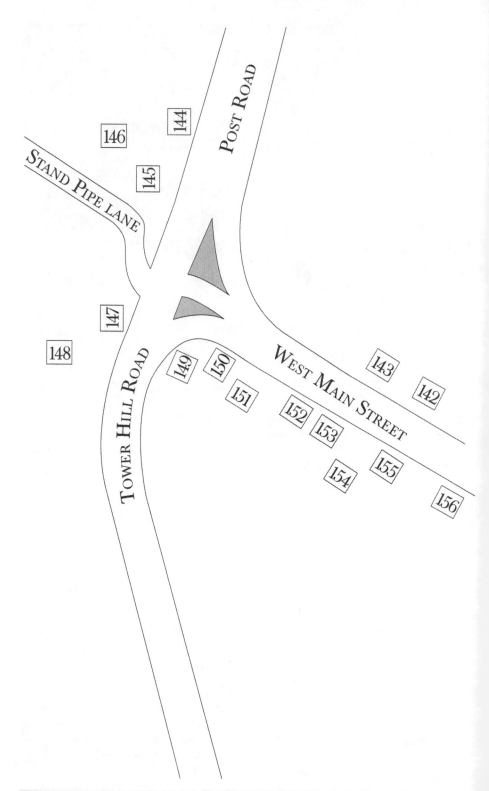

QUALITY HILL & TALBOT'S CORNER

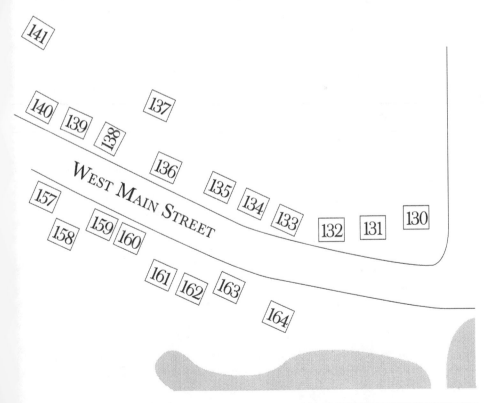

ANNA W. (HAZARD) WOOD – 1927

130.   **65 West Main Street**

This house was constructed for 21 year old Anna Wood, her husband Sherman Taylor Tourgee Wood, and their daughter, also named Anna, in 1927. Anna was born in 1906 to Edward Weeden Hazard Jr. of Peacedale and his wife Mary Abby (Gardiner) Hazard who had been born and raised here in North Kingstown. Anna's Hazard family roots extended through her father Edward Jr., who at that time lived off of investment income, her grandfather Edward Sr. who owned one of the numerous Hazard owned textile mills in the Peacedale area, her great grandfather was gentleman farmer Sylvester Robinson Hazard of Point Judith and Newport, and her great uncle was famed Newport physician Rowland Robinson Hazard. With such a well-known pedigree and such high profile relations, it is easy to understand why Anna, who had become pregnant at 15 and then married after the fact upon turning 16, was relocated out of Peacedale, a village essentially owned by her relatives, to this fine house in Wickford. Anna's troubles continued into 1928, when she divorced Sherman T. T. Wood and then married local house painter Arthur L. Pollock. It seemed that Great Depression did not affect all Hazards equally, as after 1930, Anna's father Edward Jr., who had never once listed an occupation on a census report, all of a sudden became a butcher. In 1931, Anna signed over ownership of the house to her mother Mary Abby Hazard who had it turned into a two-family home and rented the units out. After her death, the house was purchased from her estate by Roger W. Rodman.

A menu from Rodman's The Crossing.

Roger Rodman and his wife Jessie (Maglone), who lived with Jessie's parents at what is now 89 West Main Street, continued to rent out the second floor apartment, and remodeled the first floor of this house into a restaurant which they called "The Crossing" in honor of the nearby intersection of the former Sea View trolley line and West Main Street. Roger and Jesse operated "The Crossing" from 1939 until 1945. In 1945, as he was retiring, they closed the restaurant and reconfigured the building back into a one-family home. Roger and Jesse Rodman lived here until Roger's passing in 1950. After his death, Jesse sold the building to dentist Frank E. Turco.

Dr. Frank Turco had left the US Navy as a Lt. Commander in 1947 and operated a successful dental practice out of this building for more than 30 years; for 25 years of that timeframe he also served as the NK School Dept. dentist. He was active in the Wickford Lions Club and served a term as that organization's president. The building also housed Doctor Murray's office for a time, and after Turco's retirement was the office for local attorney Leo Sullivan. Although Frank Turco passed away in 1993, the building is still owned by the Turco Family.

OTHNIEL BROWN – 1805

131.   *75 West Main Street*

This home was built by house carpenter Othniel Brown on land he purchased from Thomas Capron in 1804. Brown moved into the house, which also included a standalone carpenter's shop on the same parcel, with his wife Martha (Whitehorn) and family in 1805. Little is known about Othniel Brown beyond these simple facts. In 1817, perhaps taking advantage of house building opportunities in a new area of the nation opening for settlement, Othniel Brown and his family moved to the new village of Elba, in Genesee County, New York. He lived out the remainder of his life there. He sold this house and the carpenter shop to Silas and Sarah Allen.

Very little as well, is known about Quidnessett farmer Silas Allen and his second wife Sarah who purchased the house in 1817. At this point in his life, Silas was buying and selling real estate quite regularly and this purchase may have been completed strictly as an investment. Due to the fragmented nature of North Kingstown real estate records in this time frame, it is also not clear exactly when the Allen's sold the property or whether they actually resided in it. Whatever the date might have been, the next owners of this house were Timothy Russell Peckham and his wife Sarah (Hazard) Peckham.

Timothy Peckham joined his older brother Benjamin who had already moved to Wickford from Newport, where they were both born of Benoni Peckham and Mary Lawton, decades earlier. Both brothers lived quite close to their uncle Benedict Peckham who had a large farm near what is now the intersection of

Tower Hill and Ten Rod Roads. While Benjamin chose a mariner's life, the career path of his father, Timothy's future lay in a life of farming as his uncle's did and Tim Peckham may have worked on the Benedict Peckham farm while living here in the village. In 1827, Timothy Peckham sold this house and purchased a large farm in Exeter where he remained for the rest of his days, farming it with his sons Timothy Jr. and Thomas Hazard Peckham. This house was purchased by local mariner Capt. John Nichols at that time.

Capt John Nichols and his wife Lydia, the widow of shipwright and mariner James MacKenzie and daughter of the aforementioned Benedict Peckham, lived in this house for many years. Nichols continued to go to sea throughout this time-frame and shows up in the historic record as the master of the sSchooners *Ann* and *Mary Nichols* and the sloops *Emily, Advance,* and *Helen.* The Nichols sold the house in 1843 to Jeremiah Carpenter Jr. and moved around the corner to a house on the west side of Post Road.

Jeremiah Carpenter Jr. was a second generation blacksmith who ran a black-smith shop on a parcel of land just to the east of this house with his brother-in-law Horace J. Shippee who had apprenticed under him in

1841. Their shop was called Carpenter & Shippee and was a highly successful firm. Jeremiah moved into this house with his wife Welthan (Shippee) Carpenter with whom he had two children, and later lived here with his second wife Anna (Gardiner) Carpenter, whom he married after Welthan died in 1881. Jeremiah served as a member of both the Town Council and the RI General Assembly and was a Deacon of the Wickford Baptist Church for 47 years. He was 91 years old at his death in 1903 and was one of the town's oldest and most respected residents. Prior to his death, in 1898, he sold the house to Absalom Straight.

Jeremiah Carpenter Jr.

The Jeremiah Carpenter family standing outside 75 West Main Street circa 1880.

Three ladies and a cat pose outside 75 West Main Street, circa 1890.

Ab Straight was somewhat of an anachronism, albeit a successful one, by 1898. He spent his life working as a wheelwright and cabinetmaker, and as there were few wheelwrights around as the "Age of the Automobile" began, he kept busy working on wagon wheels, doing fine cabinetry repair and other such things. He would supplement his income when required by working as a house carpenter as well. In an amazing turn of events, Absalom Straight too, was married to a woman whose maiden name was Welthan Shippee and she was indeed related to Jeremiah Carpenter's first wife. Welthan died in 1922 and Ab owned the home alone for another decade. In 1932, he sold it to an acquaintance, house carpenter John Wilcox, with the stipulation that he be allowed to live out his days here. In 1945, 90 year old Ab Straight passed away and was buried next to Welthan in the Shippee family graveyard in the Shippeetown section of East Greenwich.

House carpenter John Wilcox, his wife Ruth (McCombs) and their children moved into the house in 1932, keeping Ab Straight as a boarder here for a dozen years. In 1946, they transferred ownership of the home to their son Raymond W. Wilcox, who worked during WWII as a civilian worker at the aircraft overhaul and repair shop at Quonset Point, and then as a worker for the RI Dept. of Roads and Bridges. In 1960, the Wilcoxes sold the house to Edward and Connie Sweck and moved to Sweet Lane in nearby Allenton.

Raymond Wilcox

The Swecks made the house into a multi-family rental investment property and did not live there. In 1972, they sold it to RI School of Design professor John Lukens who restored the house and lived in the largest unit. John Lukens sold it in 1979 and its subsequent owners, the Witoska, McLoughlin, Underhill, Jones, Higgins, and DeJordy families have primarily used the building as a rental property.

ROBERT HAZARD NILES – 1804

132.   *83 West Main Street*

This house was constructed in 1804 for cabinetmaker Robert Hazard Niles on a parcel he purchased from Henry Vaughan early that year. For reasons yet unknown, Niles, who may be responsible for much of the fine colonial and early 19th century furniture in collections today that came out of the Niles family in Kingston, lived here in the house for only a short while. In January of 1806, he moved with his family to Pawtuxet village in Warwick, where he lived out the remainder of his days operating as a furniture merchant in his later years after his skills faded due to age. He sold this house to Captain Samuel Carter.

Capt. Samuel Carter, a prominent mariner, West Indies trader, and, at one time Dept. High Sheriff for the Kings (later Washington) County, was both admired and reviled during his time in this home. In 1806, at the time he purchased it, he was a prominent and respected member of the community and served in the capacity of county dept. sheriff honorably. In 1810, he seemingly hatched an elaborate plot, partnering with cargo officer Alexander Stuart to betray and defraud his friend and business partner Stukely Himesn a local merchant and fellow West Indies Trader along with countless local investors. He sailed off on the ship *Ocean*, a vessel he owned in partnership with Himes, Capt. Richard Barney, and shipwright Henry Vaughan, with a full cargo of goods ready to be traded in the Caribbean, a cargo financed, as was the ship, by numerous local investors. When Carter and Stuart reached their destination they staged what amounted to a mutiny, putting the crew off the vessel and selling, not only the cargo, but the ship as well, on the open market. The two co-conspirators split these monies and were never heard from again. Back here in Wickford, Stukely Himes was financially ruined by his friend's betrayal and had to sell off all of his assets, including his home, to cover his losses. Investors lost large sums of money as well and Carter's few remaining assets in the village were seized. When the dust settled in 1812, this house was owned by one of those investors, Benjamin Reynolds. He eventually sold it to his cousin Jonathan Reynolds who also lost money in the Carter affair. As both of these gentlemen owned their own homes, it can be assumed that the house was used as a rental property until it was sold by Jonathan to a relation in March of 1834.

That relation was William N. and Sarah (Reynolds) Tourgee. William was a house carpenter who worked locally and they moved in with their children Emeline, Mary Eliza, Rebecca, and William Jr. When William died unexpectedly in 1865, Sarah's brother Sheffield Reynolds came to his sister's rescue, buying the house from her and then gifting it back to her, thereby allowing her to have not only a lump sum of money, but a home in which to raise her family. Sheffield at that time was a successful textile mill owner who owned and operated a mill in Somerville, Connecticut. After Sarah Tourgee's death in 1878, the house which reverted back to Sheffield was sold to Horace and Eunice Hammond.

No one who was alive in 1913 would dispute the fact that old Horace Hammond, who died in Mach of that year, had left an indelible mark on the community. For certain, they'd all admit, numerous Hammonds could lay claim to that statement; why, Hammonds have had an influence upon North Kingstown since the very beginning. But none of them had done it quite like Horace. Horace Hammond was born some 78 years earlier in 1834 to Cranston and Eunice Hammond of Wickford. As a young man he was sent off to Providence to apprentice with a prominent carpenter named John Pitts. After a decade or so of working and living in the capital city, part of that time with his young wife Eunice (Slocum), he came back to Wickford and set up shop as it were. Shortly after returning to the village, he purchased this home on West Main Street and began to leave his mark on the community. His first big job was as the lead carpenter on the construction of the Chapin Bobbin Works at the corner of Brown and Boston Neck Road. This building now houses The Kayak Center and Gold Lady Jewelers among other things. After completing that he performed the same function on the construction of the impressive mill building at Belleville. He and Eunice also had a son named Edgar born to them during this timeframe. Sadly Edgar did not live to see his third birthday and even sadder still Horace and Eunice never had another child of their own. They did however, become the legal guardians of young Henry L. Morse, the son of local saloon keeper William Morse and his wife Octavia (Smith) after their family fell apart. So with a son or sorts in Henry, the Hammond family got along just fine. Horace then went on to build the Wickford National Bank Building (now the home of The Standard-Times) after its original office was destroyed by fire. His ward, young Henry, made his adoptive parents proud by being a whiz at school, eventually becoming a successful bookkeeper and marrying Hattie Belle, the daughter of Wickford Junction shopkeeper Almond E. Huling. Around this time Horace Hammond, a man who was so successful at his craft

Post card view of 83 West Main Street.

that he actually had purchased a large orange grove as an investment down in Eustis, Florida, began the job that would define him for the rest of the citizenry of Wickford. If Horace was an artist with wood and nails, well then the grand steeple, bell and clock tower he constructed for St Paul's Episcopal Church on Main Street was his masterpiece. He felt so connected to the steeple that he continued to maintain and repair it as long as he was able. Horace's life went along in a predictable fashion, filled with work and family, until 1910 when he lost his life partner Eunice. Folks remarked that he just wasn't the same after that and three years later, while on a trip to Eustis to visit his orange groves there, he passed away. He was carried past that extraordinary steeple for the last time by the folks that knew him best; the town blacksmith, a couple of fellow carpenters, a stone mason he worked with often, and a very appreciative Providence bookkeeper named Henry. No one back at the beginning of the last century had any problem remembering Horace Hammond; all one had to do was look around, his legacy was everywhere. Now, we in the next century can be reminded of him as well; each and every time we pass by one of his remarkable creations. The Hammond family sold the house in 1919 to William S. and Mary B. Lewis.

William Lewis was known to all in the village as Conductor Lewis, a moniker that referred to his long-standing career as a railroad conductor for the New York, New Haven, & Hartford Railroad at which he worked for half a century. He began as a waterboy on the trains in 1877 and worked his way through the ranks to head conductor on the Boston to New York run. He was actively involved also in the Masonic organization as well as the Order of Railroad Trainmen and the Railroad Conductors Association of America. Mary Lewis passed away in 1949 and Conductor Lewis joined here in 1955. Their heirs sold the house to the Bardsley family, who later sold it to Morris Packard.

Morris Packard, was the owner of Crafts Inc. of Providence and a member of the local art community. After his death, his family sold the house to the Deitch family. It is now owned and cared for by the Hacketts.

THE ISAAC REYNOLDS HOUSE – 1807

133.   **89 West Main Street**

This house at 89 West Main Street, formerly known as the Grand Highway, was constructed in 1807 on land purchased from Anstis Lee Updike, by Davis Mills-born carpenter Isaac Reynolds. Isaac was born in 1781 to Benjamin and Elizabeth Reynolds on the family farm on the Devil's Foot Road. The farmstead property is now occupied by the Calvary Chapel; formerly Greenmeadow Baptist Church. Isaac's sister, Mehitable, married Ezra Davis of the founding Davis clan, and throughout much of his life, Isaac worked side-by-side with his brother-in-law, a prominent area housewright. Indeed, Ezra most probably assisted Isaac with the construction of his fine home. Ezra and Isaac were involved in the construction of textile mills as well, having built and maintained the mills at Davis Mills and Sand Hill in North Kingstown as well as a number of small mills in East Greenwich and Potowomut. For

**Silhouette of
Anstis Lee Updike**

*From A History of the Episcopal
Church in Narragansett, Rhode
Island, Volume 3*

a time even, Isaac Reynolds and his father Benjamin shared ownership of one of the small mills that existed at Sand Hill Village, a small textile mill village centered around Sand Hill Pond on what is now Chadsey Road. He eventually sold that concern and using the proceeds purchased shoreline property in the newly platted Elamsville section of Wickford on what would become Brown Street. Around this time he also became part owner, along with his son Isaac Jr. and his son-in-law Harrison G. O. Gardiner, of the sloop *Commodore*, which they operated as a regular packet run between Wickford and Albany.

Isaac Reynolds constructed wharfage and warehouse space on the Brown Street property and opened one of the area's earliest lumber and construction material yards there. This lumber yard was subsequently owned by Isaac's son Stephen, then the Straight family, the Sherman Brothers, and then the Barber family and now is occupied by retail establishments including Teddy Bearskins. During this timeframe Isaac Reynolds continued to work with his brother-in-law Ezra as records (Ezra Davis accounting books) show that he provided windows, sash, trim and other construction materials to him.

Isaac Reynolds married Elizabeth Gardiner, daughter of Huling and Elizabeth Gardiner, and had three children that survived to adulthood; Isaac Jr., Stephen, and Elizabeth Frances. Capt. Isaac Reynolds Jr. chose the mariner's life and after a period of time as master of the family-owned packet run to Albany, signed on to a yet-unknown vessel working in the Triangle Trade between Rhode Island, West Africa, and the Carribbean. Isaac Reynolds Jr. died at Elmina Castle, the old Dutch Fort on the Gold Coast of Africa (now Ghana), the center of the slave trade in West Africa, at the age of 28. Stephen Reynolds lived out his life in the area and owned and operated his father's lumberyard after Isaac's death. Elizabeth Frances Reynolds married Harrison Gray Otis Gardiner, son of Willett and Abigail Gardiner, on July 18th 1841. Upon Isaac's death in January of 1864, ownership of the house passed to Elizabeth F. and Harrison G. O. Gardiner.

Harrison G. O. Gardiner was born in Hancock Massachusetts in 1814 to Willett and Abigail Gardiner. His ancestors were from this area, but his father had moved to the Hancock region when settlement opened up there soon after the Revolution. In 1827 Willett relocated his family to Moravia, NY, and Harrison stayed there until around 1839 when he returned to "the land of his father's," North Kingstown, RI, where he took up the mariner's life working on the packet run owned by his eventual father and brother-in-law. He married Elizabeth F. Reynolds in July of 1841 and commenced to live in the house with Isaac and his family. After eventually giving up the life of a merchant seaman Harrison joined his father-in-law as a carpenter and was also identified in his will as an "agriculturist." Too old to serve in the Grand Army of the Republic, during and immediately after the Civil War, Harrison G. O. Gardiner was assigned by the State Provost Marshall with the important but heartbreaking task of locating and retrieving the remains of identified Rhode Islanders for eventual burial back in their family plots. After the war, Harrison Gardiner made his mark locally as an avid genealogist and local historian and even wrote a regular feature in the predecessor paper to the Wickford Standard, the Rhode Island Telephone, called "Wickford Reminiscences," examples of which can be found on microfilm in the NK Free Library. Harrison was also a poet of sorts and his work was published in the Wickford Standard right up until his death, including the poem that accompanies his obituary. Harrison and Elizabeth had three children Isaac, Abbie, and Millard. Both Isaac and Abby died young. Millard, whose first wife had died young, made his living as a house painter. Upon Harrison's death in 1894 the house became solely owned by Elizabeth, his wife who lived there with Millard and his family. By 1896 Elizabeth had transferred ownership to Millard and his second wife; they sold it to Adelia Kenyon.

Little is known about the home's ownership by Adelia (Sherman) Kenyon and her husband Nathan beyond what can be extracted from her obituary. She apparently ran the place during the first portion of the 20th century as the Kenyon House, a boarding house/hotel. This was probably planned to take advantage of the influx of tourists brought to the village of Wickford by the Newport & Wickford Rail and Steamship Line and the Sea View Electric Trolley Line. Indeed the Wickford station of the Sea View Line was just a few hundred feet away at the present day intersection of West Main Street and Newtown Avenue. Most likely, the large front porch that graced the building for many decades was added during this timeframe. Adelia apparently also ran a dressmaking and millinery shop in Wickford in a building most probably torn down to construct the Gregory Building. After selling the house to John and Jennie Maglone in 1920, it appears that she was separated or divorced from Nathan as she lived in Richmond, RI and census data places him in East Greenwich. She had one daughter Susie Gardiner who was married to Edwin Gardiner and was carried to her grave by her son-in-law and her nephews Lodowick and Harry Shippee and Bernard Edwards.

John and Jennie (McCombs) Maglone purchased the house from Adelia Kenyon as a retirement home of sorts. Originally John farmed a large parcel of land in the Belleville section of town adjacent to Oak Hill Road and also ran a very successful ice business specializing in the delivery of icebox ice to residential and commercial properties called the Belleville Ice Company. He sold these operations in 1920 and relocated to Wickford, not only to be nearer to his two married daughters who lived in the village (who were among the very first public high school graduating class in North Kingstown), but also to concentrate on his new position on the State Board of Public Roads through which he advocated for improved as well as additional roadways here in North Kingstown. He died somewhat unexpectedly from a heart attack in 1925. Jennie Maglone, who was born in Glasgow, Scotland, lived on in the house with her son J. Gordon and his wife Kate and their family until her eventual death in May of 1932. During most of their time there, the Maglones, like the Kenyons and Gardiners before them, rented rooms to help cover costs. Indeed the 1920 census shows Sea View trolley car motorman Edwin Noyes and his wife Annie living in the house. In 1931, just prior to her death, Jennie had transferred ownership of the home to her son Gordon. Gordon and Kate, who lost their only child at an early age, continued to live in the house after Jennie's demise. J. Gordon Maglone, who worked in and retired from the University of Rhode Island maintenance department, and Kate who was one of the very first employees of the fledgling North Kingstown School Dept. lunch program in the early 1960s, owned and lived in the property and rented out rooms as their parents before them until 1967 when they retired to property they owned on the Jerry Brown Farm just south of Wakefield in South Kingstown. Later owners include the Brown, Gunnip, Hellewell, and Learned families. The house is presently owned and was recently restored by the Dacey family.

GEORGE NICHOLS – 1805

134.   ***95 West Main Street***

This house was constructed in 1805 for merchant George Nichols on a lot he had purchased from Lodowick Updike in late 1804. The style, appearance, and timeframe of this home's construction suggest it was probably built by the Holloway family. George Nichols, son of George and Rachel A. Nichols, had come to Wickford a decade earlier from East Greenwich, when his sister Polly married Wickford dry goods store owner Richard Thomas. The Thomas family sold half of a double house/store building that they owned on Main Street to George Nichols, and he opened a grocery store in the street level storefront adjacent to his sister and brother-in-law's dry goods store. Both families lived in the same building on the upper floors (for more information, see *Walking in Olde Wickford Vol. 1* – 60 Main St.). Nichols evidently decided to move into his own single-family home here in 1805, although anecdotal evidence suggests he continued to operate the Main Street store. Very little information beyond this can be discerned regarding George Nichols life other than the fact that by 1827 he was in financial difficulty and mortgaged all of his properties to local shipbuilders Christopher and Boone Spink and by 1828 was required to sell off these properties to satisfy his debtors. He sold all of his properties, the house, storefront, and a large Ten Rod Road woodlot parcel, to Erastus Fenton Knowlton. George Nichols died on July 3, 1829 and is most likely buried in the Nichols family plot in what is now part of West Greenwich.

Prominent Providence grocer Erastus Fenton Knowlton came to Wickford with his second wife Rhoda (Gage) and his daughter Rebecca, in 1828, his first wife Waite (Winsor) having perished in 1818 soon after giving birth to Rebecca. Knowlton stayed here, presumably operating the grocery store, until 1838, when his daughter married Henry Angell of Scituate. Knowlton sold off his properties at that time, with this home being purchased by Caleb and Alice Lawton of Exeter. Sadly Knowlton died of typhoid fever in 1840 soon after re-establishing himself as a Providence grocer and getting elected to the school committee there. He is buried next to his first wife in the Winsor lot in Gloucester, RI.

Caleb and Alice (Albro) Lawton were the founders of the small village of Lawtonville in Exeter; they bought this home and quickly resold it to two of their sons, Beriah and Samuel for "good will, love, and natural affection," along with $1000.00 in January of 1839. The evidence strongly suggests that Samuel and Mary (Brown) Lawton never lived in the house, staying in Exeter throughout their lives, but Beriah and Sarah (Wightman) Lawton did relocate to Wickford. In December of 1846 they purchased Samuel's half share of the property and became its sole owners. Around that same time Beriah inherited a large parcel of land from his grandfather Thomas Albro; that consisted of most of present day Cold Spring and Poplar Point. Beriah and his family eventually moved to a farm on that property and in November of 1853 sold this house to prominent Wickford merchant Horatio Nelson Reynolds.

Beriah Lawton

Proverbial bachelor Horatio N. Reynolds was a wealthy merchant and landlord when he purchased this home. He owned and operated a popular and successful general store in the village from 1833 until he turned 93 years old and was also president of the Wickford Savings Bank for many years, in addition to owning and renting out numerous properties in and around Wickford. Reynolds evidently enjoyed his role as one of the villages "most well-to-do citizens." He always dressed sharply and was known to carry a sizeable bankroll with him at all times, a habit which got him robbed on at least one occasion. As a wealthy man who never married, he often employed a live-in housekeeper who usually was a niece or some other relative. As he lived to the ripe old age of 98 years, he unfortunately outlived not only most of his relations but also nearly all of his liquid assets. He died in 1903, cash poor but land rich and much of his holdings had to be sold off to satisfy the dictates of his will and estate. This house was not sold though and was left in his will to his nephew and niece George B. & Mary Reynolds of Providence. George and Mary held on to the property for another twenty years, utilizing it as an income producing rental property. In 1923, they sold it to William and Sarah Moffitt.

Horatio N. Reynolds

William A. Moffitt continued an interesting tradition whereby most of t various owners of this house were associated with grocery and dry goods store. He came here from his birthplace in Newton, Massachusetts, to work for the Mayflower Store, one of the first chain grocery stores to open a market in North Kingstown. Later William Moffitt worked at Ryan's Market. He and his wife Sarah (Smith) raised nine children here in the house; sons William Jr., Christopher, John, Lloyd, and Raymond and daughters Evelyn, Virginia, Rita, and Gladys. William Moffitt died in 1945 and the house was left to his widow Sarah. She continued to live in the house with her son Christopher and daughter Evelyn who never married and was a popular teacher in the North Kingstown School System.

When Sarah joined her husband at Elm Grove cemetery in 1952, the house became the property of Christopher Moffitt . Christopher, who served in the US Army during WWII, was the assistant manager of the Narragansett Hotel in Providence for many years and later managed the Boxwood Inn, a fine dining restaurant formerly located in what is now the Pagoda Inn on Post Road and owned by local dentist Stanley VanWagner. At the time of his death in 1981, he was living here with school teacher Evelyn Moffitt and his widowed sister Virginia Burchell. His siblings sold the house finally in 1984 after 61 years of Moffitt family ownership. Later owners were James Barlow, Anne Ward Wallou and Karen Thorkildsen.

Evelyn Moffit

For many years, The Boxwood Inn, a fine dining restaurant on Post Road was managed by Christopher Moffitt. The Boxwood Inn was located in the space now occupied by the Pagoda Inn.

WILLIAM HOLLOWAY JR. – 1803

135.   *103 West Main Street*

This house, the first built after the 1802 platting of the area by Lodowick Updike, was constructed by house and ship wright William Holloway Jr. on a lot he purchased from Mary Updike. The earliest descriptions of the property indicate it included a "cooper's shop," a feature which was identified in 1809 when Holloway sold the parcel to the Honorable Daniel Champlin. There is no indication that William Jr. was trained as a cooper or barrel maker, so it must have been either rented out or utilized by a yet identified Holloway relation. Holloway seemingly sold the house as soon as his new house, located just west of this one, was completed.

Daniel Champlin, a well known and respected Exeter farmer and RI General Assembly Member, lived on a large farm in the Yawgoog Valley section of that community. He purchased the house as a gift for his son Benjamin Champlin, who was a Major of the 8th Regiment of the Washington County troops of the RI State Militia. Benjamin was set to marry Maria Hammond, daughter of William & Alice (Tillinghast) Hammond, and after their marriage, Maria moved into this home with her new husband. Sadly, their time together was short, as Benjamin Champlin died in September of 1814 at the age of 25. Maria left the house after his death and never remarried, living first with her parents and then spending the remainder of her days living with her sister Lydia, the widow of Jabez Bullock, in her Brown Street home. Daniel Champlin reassumed ownership of this house after his son's tragic death, and eventually sold it, in 1819, to Christopher and

Sarah (Congdon) Allen. Benjamin Champlin was posthumously given the honorary rank of Colonel and is buried with Maria in the Jabez Bullock plot in Elm Grove Cemetery.

Christopher Allen identified himself as a farmer throughout his life. The land that he and his brother Charles, who was married to Mary Congdon, sister of Christopher's wife Sarah, farmed was the Homestead Farm at Cocumscussoc, now known commonly as Smith's Castle, which their wives father Benjamin Congdon had purchased from Wilkins Updike in December of 1812, and then left to his children upon his death in 1816. Wilkins Updike had, however, included a life tenancy along with the property for Abigail Updike. As Abigail lived in the Castle until her death in 1824, there was no place for Christopher and Sarah to live at Cocumscussoc until Abigail's demise. Soon after that occurred, Christopher and Sarah Allen sold this home to Charles and Mary and presumably moved into Smith's Castle at Cocumscussoc. Charles and Mary Allen stayed here at this house until February of 1840, when they then moved to the Allen Homestead Farm in Allenton. Charles and Mary Allen then sold this house to popular local educator Francis Chappell.

Francis Chappell and his wife Bathsheba (Slocum) came to Wickford in 1815 to teach at the then renowned Washington Academy. He stayed on teaching in the same building after the Academy closed, working then for combined school districts 3 & 4 of the North Kingstown District school system. Francis retired from teaching finally in 1858 after a career of 43 years and passed away in 1860. Bathsheba died in 1861 and this house passed down to their unmarried daughter Mary Jane Chappell. Mary Jane supported herself largely by taking in boarders, many of whom were relatives. In the 1860s, she lived with her brother Gardner, who worked as a jeweler at the locket factory in the village, and another locket factory employee, Jedediah Fuller and his family. In the 1870s, she rented half the house out to her sister and brother-in-law James and Rhoda (Chappell) Eldred and their daughter Hannah. James Eldred previously had not only owned the locket factory that employed so many Wickford residents before the Civil War, but also lived in the fine home "The Oaklands" off of what is now Boston Neck Road with his family. Also living here in the 1870s was Mary Jane's other sister Esther who was the widow of Esbon Sanford. James Eldred also employed a live-in servant Christina White who lived here with her 6 year old daughter Cornelia. Christina White, a freed slave from Virginia, would shortly marry Jim Chase, another freed slave from Maryland and

Christina (White) Chase with her children, Cornelia White and William H. Chase.

Jim would adopt Christina's daughter "Nellie" who was purported to have been fathered by her mother's former master. Mary Jane Chappell died in 1874 and the house then became the property of James and Rhoda Eldred who continued to live here with Esther. Hannah Eldred married the Reverend Daniel Goodwin; the priest at St. Paul's Episcopal Church and was living in the rectory located across the street from her childhood home "The Oaklands." James and Rhoda also rented rooms to James Thomas, a local store clerk and his wife Eliza. Sadly, Hannah (Eldred) Goodwin died suddenly in 1877, and James Eldred passed away in 1883. Rhoda continued in the house for a time, but in 1886 sold it to her former son-in-law, Rev. Daniel Goodwin who had retired from his final church pastorate at St. Luke's in East Greenwich.

Rev. Daniel Goodwin
Courtesy St. Luke's Episcopal Church Archives

Daniel Goodwin, who came to Wickford from Bangor, Maine in 1869, was beloved in both the communities of Wickford and East Greenwich. Goodwin, who only served in the village for five years, was instrumental in the construction of the Church's signature bell and clock tower, the enlargement of the chapel, the reconfiguration of the interior of the Church, and the initiation of the project to have the simple frosted glass windows of St. Paul's replaced with the extraordinary stained glass memorial windows extant today. Goodwin was well known as a Church historian and eventually edited, revised and corrected *The History of the Episcopal Church of Narragansett, Rhode Island* written originally in 1847 by Wilkins Updike. In 1919, an ailing Daniel Goodwin sold his retirement home to John Maglone. He passed away two years later and is buried in the cemetery at St. Luke's Church in East Greenwich. His beloved Hannah rests eternal in her parents plot at Elm Grove in North Kingstown.

Both John Maglone, and the house's next owner Joseph W. Greene seemed to have purchased it speculatively as neither one owned it for even a full year. In 1921, Greene sold the home to Frank A. Peckham. Frank Peckham was born in Newport, RI, in 1860 and spent his working life in retail, working first in Newport at a hardware store, then at the Sheppard Company in Providence and then as a buyer for two different retailers in New Haven, Connecticut. In 1898, he took his savings and purchased the long-running Wickford business, the A. M. Thomas Dry Goods Store, and ran it as Peckham's Dry Goods. He ran this business for nearly 50 years, rarely missing a day of work until just a few before his death. He was married to Sarah McNamara also of Newport and had two sons Harold and

Frank A. Peckham and his wife Sarah McNamara.

Frank A. Peckham standing outside Peckham's Dry Goods Store.
In 1898, he purchased the business, and moved his family to Wickford.

Frank A. Peckham standing outside 103 West Main Street.

Harold
Dexter
Peckham

Frank, and two daughters, Marion and Gertrude. Frank Peckham was very active at St. Paul's Church serving as Treasurer, then Jr. and Sr. Wardens. He died in February of 1947. The house stayed in the Peckham family through Sarah's life, eventually becoming the property of son Harold Peckham who was a WWI veteran and longtime employee of a Texas-based oil company. When Harold died in 1976, the house became the property of his unmarried sister Marion who sold it to molecular biologist and Brown University professor Richard Ellis. Ellis who lived immediately west of this house in 115 West Main Street, used it as a rental property. In 1997 it was sold to its present owner Doctor John Machata.

RUFUS SWEET – 1842

136.   *115 West Main Street*

This handsome, Greek-Revival, 2½ story, 3-bay end gable house with Ionic portico has perhaps one of the most intriguing string of owners found in any home in the village of Wickford. Its first owner was master tailor Rufus Sweet and his wife Mary Ann (Congdon) Sweet. They had the home constructed on a lot they purchased from Joseph and Abigail (Updike) Reynolds, the lot having been inherited by Abigail from her father. This large and fine home was both a testimony to the skill and success of Rufus Sweet as a tailor and the concentrated wealth in the village of Wickford at that time capable of so ably supporting Sweet's business. Most certainly Sweet's clothing, sewn here in the house, was worn by the merchants, bankers, and sea captains that lived in Wickford's many fine homes. The Sweet family lived here until 1866; at that time they worked out a house swap with Syria Vaughan who owned the smaller Very home across the street.

Syria Vaughan was one of southern Rhode Island's most important businessmen, an innovative entrepreneur who dominated the late 19th century in the region. He was not only the founder of the Hamilton Web Company, a large textile manufacturing concern just south of Wickford and the "father of the narrow weave textile industry in New England," but also a savvy businessman who left the textile trade only to get in on the ground floor of the coal distribution business in the region as it supplanted both wood and water as the primary energy source available to both business and residential consumers in North Kingstown and beyond. Syria, and his wife Louise (Hamilton) Vaughn, after whom both the mill and its surrounding village was named, lived here until 1875 when they sold the house to Providence business tycoon Parley Mathewson.

Parley Mason Mathewson was born, raised, and educated in the village of East Killingly, CT. He lived there from his birth on August 31, 1813, until shortly after his fifteenth birthday. It was then and there that he began his business career, at a store of the Scituate Company which was owned by Philip Allen, a member of the rich and influential Allen family of Providence, RI. Parley was a bookkeeper, and obviously a good one, because it wasn't long before he was transferred to the Allen's main office in the heart of Providence. Before long he was the Allen's head bookkeeper and it was said that he set up a systematic method of bookkeeping for them that increased the efficiency of their many businesses and in turn their profits. His rapid ascension through the ranks of the Allen's businesses gave him the confidence to set out on his own, so he left their employ and opened up a grocery business on the corner of North Main and Waterman. Again, his business talents served him well, and before too much time had passed Mathewson's small grocery store was transformed into a successful grocery wholesale operation. His business was so good in fact, that by the early 1860s he was able to sell his business and effectively retire before he had reached his forty-fifth birthday; a remarkable achievement for the middle of the nineteenth century. At the outbreak of the Civil War, Parley Mathewson was living the life of leisure, travelling throughout the south seeking "health and pleasure." It would seem that Mathewson's incredible business sense was at work as well, because by the close of the war his knowledge of the land "Where cotton is King" served him in good stead as he then began his second, and even more successful, career as a cotton broker. By war's end the infrastructure of the Deep South was in a shambles; golden opportunities awaited any businessman with the acumen necessary to seize them. Parley Mathewson was just such a man. The emerging south had plenty of cotton and the industrial north (The Rhode Island area included) had many fabric mills just waiting to churn out cloth; all that was needed was the financing and infrastructure to bring the two together. Parley Mathewson was one of the many savvy businessmen who jumped in to fill that gap. Before long, big-time cotton broker Parley Mathewson became a mill owner as well; he owned one mill outright and had a financial interest in many others. Along the way, he acquired a fine home in Providence at 69 Angell Street, a wife Lucy, of the Capron family of the city, and three children. As the last quarter of the nineteenth century began, Parley was living the American dream, he was a huge success, a man of means; a man, who by this time was also the President of the "Third National Bank," a City Councilor, and, quite frankly, a person with a substantial disposable income. This is where North Kingstown comes into the story. Like many influential people of his time, Parley had become acquainted with and enamored of Wickford through its wonderful train and steamship connection to Newport. As so many did, he fell in love with the place while passing through it. When he was looking for an appropriate location for a "summer estate" for his immediate and extended family, Wickford was his choice. He purchased, not one, but two of the "Quality Hill's" finest homes. They were situated on adjacent lots and the two houses, along with the land and outbuildings associated with them, became the Parley Mathewson Estate. The big house was the Rufus Sweet House. It had been, prior to its purchase by Mathewson, the home of a man he was surely acquainted with, local mill magnate Syria H. Vaughan. The smaller house was the J. Adams House; it had been more recently constructed, sometime after the middle of the 1800s. The estate also included a large carriage house which has, in recent times, been remodeled into a home. Parley Mathewson's remarkable life ended on January 4, 1890 in his Angell Street home after a short illness. Although his family continued to visit the summer estate after his death, it must not have been the same without his powerful presence. Finally, in 1910, Parley Mathewson's son sold the house to a local man, Frank E. Brown.

Frank Brown, son of local blacksmith Oliver Brown, moved into the house with his wife Mary Helen (Peirce) Brown and their family. Ironically, Frank previously worked for Rufus Sweet's son Daniel, selling a full line of insurance products to the residents of the region. When Daniel Congdon Sweet retired, Frank Brown purchased the insurance company and then later purchased the home that Daniel had grown up in. In 1917, they sold the house, after their children moved out and it was too big for their needs, to Richard P. Jenks.

Richard P. Jenks purchased this house with his wife Helena. Jenks was a founding partner in the Providence based construction and engineering firm Jenks & Ballou, a business he established in 1914 with partner Henry Ballou. They were responsible for the design and construction of the massive Providence Fruit & Produce warehouse complex, the imposing South Street Power Generating Plant, portions of the Quonset/Davisville complex and a host of other buildings and structures. They sold this house in 1925 to Benjamin A. Jackson.

Advertisement for Wickford Hill Antique Shop run by Benjamin Jackson.

Benjamin Arnold Jackson bought this property as his retirement home. He had recently left a long career at the George Claflin Company of Providence, a highly successful wholesale pharmaceutical distribution company, at which he rose to Vice President and Board member. At the same time, his brother Russell Southwick Jackson, also retired from Claflin where he worked as a clerk, rented the adjacent house just to the west of this one. Ben Jackson's vocation may have been pharmacy related, but his avocation was antiques and he took up the trade of antique dealer as soon as he moved into this home. He continued in this second career until his death in 1936. At that time, the house came into the possession of the man who replaced him at the Claflin Company, company secretary and vice-president Ralph D. Kettner. The Kettners owned the property until 1944, when they sold it to George C. Cranston Jr.

George C. Cranston Jr. was the director of the Cranston's of Wickford Funeral Home located diagonally across the street. He not only ran the business, but also served as the Town of North Kingstown Tax Collector and Town Moderator while living here in the house with his wife Marjorie (Main) Cranston and their four children. In 1958, after his children had grown up and were in homes of their own, and after his mother, who lived in the residence section of the funeral home proper, passed away, he sold this house and moved into the funeral home, which was also occupied by his unmarried sister Louise. Cranston sold the house to Robinson C. Locke who resold it in 1962 to local educator John Charles.

John Charles, who finished his career as the guidance counselor at nearby Wickford Jr. High School, lived in the house until 1969. Its next owner was molecular biologist and popular Brown University professor Richard Ellis who lived in the house for twenty-five years. In 1994, he sold it to its present owner, friend and professional colleague Clarence C. Goertemiller, who was a biology professor and the head of the pre-med program at the University of Rhode Island.

The Cranston family posed outside 115 West Main Street

SYRIA VAUGHAN
CARRIAGE HOUSE – CIRCA 1871

137.   ***125 West Main Street***

This building was constructed as a stable and carriage house for the property at 115 West Main Street during the timeframe in which that fine home was owned by Syria Vaughan. It is not evident on the 1870 Wickford street map, but is specifically mentioned in the 1875 deed of transfer between Vaughan and Parley Mathewson. Additionally, it is readily apparent on the wonderful "1888 Bird's Eye View of Wickford," looking remarkably the same as it does today, although it is in that rendering, topped with an attractive cupola which was lost in the 1938 hurricane. From its initial construction date in the early 1870s through 1944 it served as a stable/carriage house and later barn/garage for all of the owners of 115 West Main Street. For details on those individuals, reference the entry for the Rufus Sweet House.

1888 Bird's Eye View of Wickford

After the 1944 purchase of the property by George Cyrus Cranston Jr., significant changes were made to the structure. As Cranston kept all of his vehicles in a garage behind his funeral home property on the other side of West Main Street, he had no real need for a large garage building such as this. He therefore had the building remodeled into a two unit rental property renting it out as an additional source of income. Among the many local people who rented here was beloved furniture dealer Zeke Harris and his wife Annie. In late 1960, after her graduation from Springfield College, George Cranston allowed his youngest daughter A. Lenore Cranston to move into the first floor unit of this building. Upon his death in 1963, ownership of the building was transferred to her.

In the fall of 1961, Lenore began her nearly thirty year teaching career at North Kingstown High School and back then, women's athletics were little more than a token afterthought overshadowed by the more "important" pursuits of the High School boys' programs. Sure girls could utilize the fields for games and practices, as long as they didn't interfere with any boys' activities. And heck, the little ladies could certainly use the boys' programs cast-off equipment if they wanted and if we have any funds left after fulfilling the needs of those boys' programs, you bet you can pick up a few items. Well, Coach Cranston would have none of that; slowly and tenaciously, behind the scenes she turned heads and changed minds. North Kingstown, guided by her vision, began its journey towards equality in school athletics long before any mention of "Title IX." Another problem of the times was the fact that there existed no vehicle in the state to allow young high school women to compete inter-scholastically. With the

A young Lenore Cranston poses with her niece and nephew, one of whom grew up to write this book.

assistance of a number of like-minded coaches in schools across the state, Lenore helped form the RI interscholastic women's league in 1971. She then proceeded to place North Kingstown Girls' Teams at the forefront in each and every sport available, winning countless divisional titles and state championships. If that was not enough, she got in on the ground floor of the formation of the Town's much admired and highly successful Recreation program and made certain that young women got equal opportunities.

Don't think that people didn't start to take notice. Lenore has already been honored by her Alma Mater's URI, when she was awarded the 1980 Coach of the Year Award and Springfield College as well as the RI Girls' Interscholastic League, who also named her Coach of the Year. In 1991, the RI Women in Sports Award was officially renamed the A. Lenore Cranston Award and has been presented ever since to a woman who most typifies the ideals that Coach Cranston personified. On December 16, 2003, the Town of North Kingstown honored her when the Main Gym at the new High School was renamed "The A. Lenore Cranston Gymnasium." And in May of 2005 Lenore was inducted into the RI Interscholastic League Hall of Fame. She passed away in March of 2006 and was mourned by the whole community. In 2007 the house was sold by her estate to one of her star athletes from the 1970s, Laurie Cason.

JEDEDIAH RATHBUN – 1853

138.   *131 West Main Street*

The two houses on this lot were constructed in 1853 for local brick mason Jedediah L. Rathbun on land he had purchased from Abigail (Updike) Reynolds. Jedediah and his wife Emeline (Tourgee) Rathbun and their twins Philander and Philena moved into the house located right on the street and Jed's mother Elizabeth, the widow of Baldwin Rathbun, lived in the back house. Both houses were most likely constructed by Emeline's father William N. Tourgee, a house carpenter who lived a few houses east of here, also on West Main Street, with whom they had lived prior to occupying these homes. Jedediah had plenty of work here in North Kingstown during this timeframe with the expansion of the textile industry here, and his son Philander apprenticed under him during this period. In 1865, this entire extended family relocated to Providence, probably following work available to the, by then, father and son bricklaying team, and sold the houses to John A. Adams.

John Adams was a Providence County thread manufacturer, who lived for most of the year in a home near Smithfield, RI. He apparently bought this property as a summer house. Although real estate records are unclear, it appears that in the early 1870s he defaulted upon his purchase agreement with the Rathbuns and the property returned to their control. It was placed back on the market and was purchased by Alfred Young, son of Wickford apothecary Eliphalet Young. He resold it quite quickly to Parley Mathewson in 1875.

Jedediah and Emeline (Tourgee) Rathbun's gravestones at Elm Grove.

Parley Mathewson remodeled the front house quite extensively, changing the roof from its original simple peaked line to a mansard roof, thereby expanding the usable space on the second floor, and adding the porch in the process. He used the front house as a guest house for his expansive summer estate here and utilized the back house as caretaker/servants quarters. For more details on Parley Mathewson, see the entry for 115 West Main Street. The Mathewson family retained ownership of his Wickford estate well after his death and finally sold the entire parcel to Frank E. Brown in 1910.

Frank Brown retained ownership of the entire Parley Mathewson Estate until 1917, living throughout that timeframe in the big house at 115 West Main St. He began his business career in the insurance industry, but later branched out into real estate investment and later banking, eventually becoming President of the Wickford Savings Bank. He also found time to serve on the board of trustees of the NK Free Library for 24 years and as a member of the Town's School Committee for 26 years. In 1917, after his children had become adults and moved out of his house, he sold the big house at 115 West Main and moved into Parley Mathewson's old guest house with his wife Mary Helen (Peirce) Brown. He rented out the back house throughout the full period of time he owned it. Upon his death in late 1943, schools were closed for a half day to honor his memory and the Town Council ordered all flags in town to fly at half staff. His wife Mary Helen stayed in this house until 1958 when she sold it to John P. Bergeron.

John Bergeron was a cartographer for the Army Corps of Engineers when he moved into the house. The former WWII Army veteran, who was a Bronze Star recipient, lived here with his wife Isabel and three children until 1962. He sold it to University of Rhode Island Political Science professor George Goodwin Jr. who lived here for only three years. In 1965, Goodwin sold the house to Fenton E. Batton.

Fenton Batton

Fenton Batton, was born in Biloxi, Mississippi, and spent his early adult years in Brattleboro, Vermont where he practiced law. The onset of WWII saw him serving in the US Navy, through which he became acquainted with Wickford. At war's end he returned to Vermont, but in 1949, he relocated with his family to Rhode Island when he took a position in the insurance industry with the General Adjustment Bureau. He initially lived in a home in the village on Main Street, but in 1965, he moved up the hill with his wife Mary Grace and their children to this house. Fenton was actively involved in both the Main Street Association in the village and the Cocumscussoc Association, the group that holds stewardship over nearby Smith's Castle. He will, however, be remembered largely for not only his vibrant and unique personality, but also his instrumental role in the founding of the Wickford Yacht Club. Fenton always claimed that the real impetus for the founding of the Wickford Yacht Club came from his wife Mary Grace who felt strongly that "children who live by the sea ought to learn how to sail." This idea, shared by NK High School teacher and friend Ralph Vale, was the driving motivation that led to their shared desire to form a sailing club. This concept met with much local enthusiasm, and the sailing club focused on training young people to sail became the Wickford Yacht Club. For more information on the history of the Wickford Yacht Club and its founding, please read the informative "History of the Wickford Yacht Club" found in print and on the group's website. Fenton Batton retired from his insurance law career in 1971 and soon after undertook a whole new vocation as a professional print model specializing in "salty seadog" and "crusty curmudgeon-like" characters, along with his forte, Santa Claus. Fenton, who had agents in both New York and Boston, found work in print advertisements for clients such as Nestles Chocolate, Herman Survivors work boots and the Polaroid Corporation. He worked successfully as a print model until well into his eighties. Fenton Batton will always be remembered as a stand-out character in a village chock full of characters. The Batton's sold this house in 1974 to Walter A. Brown. The Browns resold the house in 1977 to Community College of RI psychology professor Gerard E. Brousseau. Since 1988 the two houses and stable building have been lovingly maintained by Henry B. Spencer.

WILLIAM HOLLOWAY – 1808

139.   *141 West Main Street*

William & Mary (Eldred) Holloway purchased this parcel of land from Mary Updike in 1807 and had the home constructed soon afterward. As the Holloway family was involved in home and ship building they may have also been the builders. William Holloway Sr. identified himself as a "merchant" but it is also known that he was actively involved in the extensive maritime industry existing in Wickford village at the time. He was an owner of the sloop *Alice* and the brig *Canton* and was also thought to be involved in vessel construction with his son David. Holloway most probably used these vessels to buy and sell goods overseas. Two of Holloway's sons, William Jr. and Eldred, were merchant seamen, with William eventually rising to the rank of captain and Eldred, a mate aboard the brig *Crawford* on which he was assassinated under mysterious circumstances. Son David was a housewright and ship builder by trade and also part owner of his brother's locally renowned packet *Resolution.* William Holloway Sr. and his sons can be considered one of the most important family groups involved in the history of this phase of Wickford's existence.

William Hazard Gardiner and his wife Patience (Hendrick) Gardiner purchased the home from Isaac Briggs and his wife Lucy (Holloway) Briggs in July of 1846. Gardiner was a successful carpenter who lived in both North Kingstown and Exeter prior to the home's purchase. He was able to move into this substantial Wickford home after his wife received a substantial inheritance of monies and land upon the death of her maternal grandfather Peleg Arnold of North

Kingstown. William Gardiner continued to work as a carpenter and also served as a Captain in the 4th Company RI State Militia. He died on January 20th 1863 of cancer. The house was sold to the Congdons after the death of Patience Gardiner.

The elder Joseph Congdon had been born in 1805 in Newport but had spent much of his childhood and youth here in Wickford surrounded by the numerous Congdon relations that called North Kingstown home. He went to sea at an early age and worked his way up through the ranks until he became the master of Nantucket based whale ships. He spent five years at the Captain of the whale ship *Pacific*, four years on the whaler *James Lopez*, and seven years in charge of the grand ship *Alpha*, seen here in a rendering owned now by the Nantucket Historical Society. His sixteen years at sea were spent primarily in the Indian and Pacific Oceans and all those years were parceled out into voyages that might last as long as two years at a stretch. During those years he called Nantucket home and managed to raise a family there with his wife Phebe. In 1869, the retired sea captain returned to Wickford and purchased the big Main Street home. He and Phebe lived out there days here and are buried in Elm Grove.

You can bet that a frequent visitor to the comfortable home of Joseph and Phebe Congdon was their son Joseph William who remained on Nantucket after

Ship *Alpha* passing St. Paul's Isle Indian Ocean - November the 1st 1846, attributed to George Marshall.

Courtesy the Nantucket Historical Society

his parents moved here. During the Civil War he was the master of the gunship *Housatonic*, a 1930 ton behemoth bristling with cannon. While on blockade service off the coast of Charleston, *Housatonic* became the first vessel to be sunk by a submarine when the Confederate sub *Hunley*, which was recently raised from the depths of the Atlantic and is being restored, brought her down. After his term of service during the war, Joseph William joined the Revenue Cutter Service (RCS), the predecessor to the US Coast Guard, as the master of the cutter *Dexter* based out of New Bedford. He eventually rose to the position of Chief Training Officer for the RCS and also was involved as supervisor over the construction of the cutters *Seminole* and *McCulloch*. He too spent his final days in Wickford and is buried in Elm Grove in the same lot as his parents.

Portrait of Jesse Jay Burge
by Abbott H. Thayer, circa 1880
Courtesy the Brooklyn Museum, Gift of Jesse Jay Burge and Marie Louise Burge

Marie Louise & Jessie Jay Burge, unmarried daughters of Dr. J. H. Hobart Burge of Brooklyn, NY, purchased the house from Marianna Congdon & Ida (Congdon) Page in October of 1922. The Burge sisters were the granddaughters of Reverend Lemuel Burge who had been a long time Rector at the Old Narragansett Church in Wickford. They lived with their parents until Doctor Burge's death in 1901 and thereafter "kept house" for their brother the Reverend F. W. Burge at six different Episcopal parishes in the State of New York across a period of 21 years. They were both educated at the Packer Collegiate Institute in Brooklyn Heights, with Marie undertaking additional studies at Vassar. Jessie Burge was renowned as a violinist and also wrote poetry which she self-published on occasion. Marie Burge identified herself as a lecturer who spoke on subjects such as philosophy, history and classical literature.

When the Burge sisters moved into the home, they openly declared their intentions to "live in the style of their grandfather Rev. Lemuel Burge." To this aim, they had all modern conveniences removed from the home and spent the next thirty years living in a house heated only by fireplaces and lit only by oil lamps. Additionally, they utilized, right up until their death, the privy in the backyard rather than enjoy the conveniences of indoor plumbing. Indeed this appears to be the last home in the entire village to install a modern bathroom. Jessie Burge died in 1948 at the age of 81 and Marie in 1952 at the age of 87. They are both buried in Greenwood Cemetery in Brooklyn, NY.

Virginia Hibbard inside 141 West Main Street after renovations.

After the death of Marie Burge in 1952, the house has changed hands many times. Sam and Virginia Hibbard purchased it from the Burge estate and lovingly and faithfully restored the home's exterior and interior, returning the electricity and plumbing removed by the Burge sisters three decades earlier. Virginia Hibbard was a natural and exquisite decorator and brought elegance back to the home not seen since the days of the Congdons. They sold it in 1954 and went on to restore numerous New England homes, with their final restoration project being "Sundown," a grand circa 1785 home in North Wolfeboro NH owned by their daughter and son-in law Peter and Leigh Roessigier. From 1954 on, the next owner of this house were the Neidlingers. The Richmond, Packard and Potter families all owned it for various lengths of time. It was next owned by Wickford Baptist Church minister Weldon DeMeurers, followed by the Driscolls and Dallingers. In 1990 it was purchased by renowned 20th/21st century cabinetmaker Jeffrey Greene who presently operates his formerly Wickford based furniture shop in Newport RI. The Greenes lived here for twelve years and then sold it to the Buckley family. Since 2006 it has been owned and maintained by the Donohues.

Susan Eldred Holloway – 1843

140.   *151 West Main Street*

This house was constructed in 1843 for spinster sisters Susan and Mary Holloway, unmarried daughters of ship and housewright William Holloway and his wife Mary (Eldred) Holloway. It was constructed on one of a number of land parcels given to Susan by her father and was most probably constructed, in the Greek Revival style, by Susan and Mary's brother David who, like his father, was an accomplished house builder and shipwright. Although the house was clearly always owned by Susan Holloway, her elderly parents spent their final years living here with their daughters after selling their own home, located immediately to the east of this house, in 1846. William Holloway passed away on the 4th of July 1854 at the age of 86 years old, and Mary joined him at Elmgrove Cemetery on Thanksgiving of 1865 in her 91st year. The sisters made a comfortable living on an income that consisted of the proceeds of their work as seamstresses and milliners, which they did out of the house, lease income from the surrounding land which they let out to their brother George who was a successful farmer, and the occasional sale of a building lot from amongst the frontage parcels they owned along "The Grand Highway," now known as Main/West Main Streets. They both lived their entire lives here with Mary passing on in 1878 at the age of 71 and Susan joining her and her parents in the family plot in 1901 at almost the exact same age as her mother had been. The house was purchased from her estate by her nephew Frank L. Holloway.

Proverbial bachelor, dandy, and gadabout Frank Holloway had been a successful jewelry wholesaler in New York City and had come back to his hometown of Wickford to "retire" to a life as a real estate agent and speculator. He owned, purchased or inherited a number of Holloway family properties in the village and lived here for a number of years. He was described as "tall, good looking, and an immaculate dresser, who did a little boating and always owned a fine car." He sold this house in 1914 to Alphonso and Susan Shippee, ending 71 years of continuous Holloway ownership.

Sadly, the Shippee's ownership of the house was very short lived as Alphonso Shippee died unexpectedly less than a year after purchasing it. The house, which was to be the Quidnessett farmer's retirement home, was sold and Susan moved into a West Warwick triple-decker with her son Charles. Susan sold the house to Thomas W. and Harriet (Sunderland) Peirce.

Tommy W., as he was commonly known, to avoid confusion with his cousin Thomas J. Peirce who was the Town Clerk, was "the law" in North Kingstown at this point in time and indeed served as Chief of Police for North Kingstown, Town Sergeant, and Deputy Sheriff for Washington County, all concurrently. His wife Harriet was the daughter of popular local physician Dr. Robert Sunderland. They lived here essentially the rest of their days with Tommy W. dying in 1926 and Harriet passing away in her son-in-law and daughter's house just two doors down the street in 1949. Daughter Mary Helen (Peirce) Brown and her husband Frank sold the house in 1944 after Harriet moved in with them. The house was owned for a short time by both the Alan Grinstead and Emanuel Taylor families until it was sold to perhaps its most locally "famous" owners, two widowed sisters Frankie Ross and Oda Metz.

You see, from 1947 to 1977, Frances "Frankie" Ross and her sister Oda Metz and their guest house were a part of the scene here in the village. Frankie and Oda came to Wickford Village as a result of tragic circumstances. Within the span of a few short months, both of the sisters' husbands passed away, leaving them alone. They came to Wickford to be near another sister that already lived here on West Main Street and decided to stay. They purchased the West Main Street home in 1947 and came up with a plan to run a boarding home in it to support

Guests enjoying a meal at the Metzi-Ross Guest House.

themselves. They came up with the name Metzi-Ross because it sounded a lot like Betsy Ross, something that folks would have an easy time remembering; and remember it they did. For thirty years, the "No Vacancy" sign was more often than not hanging out front. The place was utilized not only by a steady stream of tourists who would come year after year and utilize one or more of the five rooms that they rented out, but also by a never ending string of Navy personnel who were here for either a short time for training or stayed at Metzi-Ross while they searched for more permanent housing elsewhere.

Oda and Frankie both had their duties to perform. Oda was in charge of what went on inside and the more out-going Frankie, who had a driver's license, ran around town as need be. Both women were actively involved in the goings-on at the First Baptist Church in Wickford and the Order of Eastern Star, a Masonic related women's organization which met at the Masonic Temple on Ten Rod Road.

Things at the Metzi-Ross Guest House came to an end in 1977, with the massive scale down of personnel at Quonset/Davisville and the death of Oda Metz the year before. Frankie stayed in town until she passed away in March of 1986. Both women were buried out of state back with their respective husbands. They were fixtures here in Wickford, and sometimes as I walk by their old home, I can almost see them sitting there on the front porch whiling away the hours

as they wait for another guest to arrive. Frances Ross sold the house to Doctor Richard Croteau, who lived here with his family and ran his doctor's office out of the first floor. In 1987, the Croteaus sold the home to its present owners the Galster family, who restored it back into a single family home. The Metzi-Ross Guest House sign, hangs proudly over an interior mantelpiece.

The Metzi-Ross Guest House

HOLLOWAY BARN/FRED HORSFALL – CIRCA 1843/1923

141.   ***159 West Main Street***

This building was constructed sometime after 1843 and served as a barn/ stable/carriage house for the Holloway sister's house just to its southeast. During this timeframe it was owned and utilized by the Holloway family, the Alphonso Shippee family, and for a time, Thomas W. Peirce and his family. In 1923, Thomas W. Peirce subdivided his property and created a separate lot which had frontage on West Main Street and included this building. That parcel, whose description detailed a building and related structures but no house, was purchased by Fred W. Horsfall, who raised the barn up onto a brick foundation and converted it into a home.

Fred Horsfall was the son of English immigrants, and his parents came here to work in the textile mills of North Kingstown. His mother Rosanna (Coyle) Horsfall died three months after his birth and he was largely raised by his uncle and aunt, William and Clarrissa Horsfall, who had also come here to work in the mills. Fred too, spent his life working in various textile mills including Belleville, where he worked as a weaver, and Hamilton Web, a place at which he finished his working career, first as a foreman in the weaving department and then as the overseer of the

Fred Horsfall

mill's shipping department. He and his wife Martha (Caufield) were sadly child-less. Fred was an avid musician, during one period leading his own orchestra, and for years gave piano lessons from his home. He was extraordinarily active in numerous fraternal organizations including the Masons, the Shriners, the Odd Fellows, the Royal Arcanum, and the Eastern Star. He was busy at St. Paul's Episcopal Church in the village, singing in the choir, and serving as a vestryman and a church warden. Martha died in 1950 and Fred in 1954. The house was purchased from his estate by Paul H. St. Pierre.

Paul St. Pierre, was a Northeastern University educated electrical engineer, who had prior to this, been living in surplus Navy rental property in the Wickford Housing Project utilized by the Quonset/Davisville Naval Base. He moved into this house with his wife Margaret (Towne) and children Jean and John. He spent his entire career working for the Narragansett Electric Company, eventually rising to head of the engineering department. He was a long time member of the Narragansett Archaeological Society and was considered one of the region's premier amateur archaeologists. Upon his death, his extensive collection of

Paul St. Pierre

artifacts was donated to RI College. He was an award winning amateur photographer and member of the Providence Camera Club and he additionally served for many years on the North Kingstown Planning Commission, much of that time as chairperson. He was also my grandfather and stepped up to fill the shoes of my father when he died at an early age. He was the best man I ever knew. He sadly succumbed to Alzheimer's disease in 1994. Upon his death the house was sold to Francis Reis Sr.

Francis Reis was a WWII US Navy veteran who spent his career after service working as a civil service worker in the supply department at Quonset Point Naval Air Station. He also served in the Coast Guard Auxiliary. He passed away in 2006 and the home is still owned by members of the Reis family.

THOMAS LEWIS – 1896

142.   ***181 West Main Street***

This home was constructed in 1896 for Thomas Lewis, the youngest of the five fishing Lewis brothers, on land he purchased from his brother Isaac. Married to Sarah Gardiner, Tom Lewis along with his brothers John, George, Fred, and Bill, were owners of the unique fishing vessel *Lewis Brothers*, which they used for decades in their careers as highly successful trap

Tom Lewis

fisherman. Their fishing smack, *Lewis Brothers* was constructed with a "live fish hold" which allowed them to bring their catch each day still alive and flapping to whatever fish market, from Boston to New York City and anywhere in between, that was paying the highest price. Tom, and all of his brothers, did well, and all raised families here in Wickford. Tom Lewis fished for nearly all of his life and died at the age of 86 years old in 1952 as the last of the Lewis Brothers. Ten years prior, in 1942, he sold his home to William "Willie" Boone Babcock.

Willie Boone Babcock was born in 1873 on the family farm on Quidnessett Neck. This farm, known as the Nicholas Spink farm, had been in his mother's family for many decades and Willie represented the eighth generation to farm the land. Sadly, he was also the last, as in the early 1940s the US Government condemned his land and all of it around him for the construction of the Quonset/Davisville military complex. Willie, who also ran a clambake business on the property and was known as one of the premier bakemasters in South County, took what money was given him by the US Navy and purchased this home and began a new life as a successful insurance agent for National Grange Insurance Company. William Boone Babcock, who was also known to proudly proclaim an unsubstantiated ancestral connection to pioneer Daniel Boone, was a founding member of the Quidnessett Grange and served as master of the RI State Granges from 1934 to 1938. He and his wife Annie Reynolds, daughter of Allen Reynolds, an influential textile mill owner in Davisville, never had any children. Willie died in 1952; in

Courtesy the North Kingstown Free Library Collection

William Boone Babcock

Vintage postcard view of the Tom Lewis home.

1956 his house was sold to Gene Sawyer, who quickly resold it to John R. M. Phelan.

Doctor John Phelan was one of the areas earliest psychiatrists and operated an office here for four years, in 1961, he sold the house to Doctor Bohdan Kusma who lived in the house with his family and practiced pediatric medicine from the first floor office created in the house by Phelan. Dr. Kusma was born and educated in the Ukraine and told a harrowing tale of how he and his wife and small children escaped from that region just as the Soviet "Iron Curtain" fell across Eastern Europe. He practiced medicine here in Wickford until 1970 when he became a well-respected member of the staff of Women's and Infants Hospital in Providence. He sold the house to URI physics professor Charles Kaufman who owned it until 1979. Since then it has been owned by a succession of dentists who have shared practice space on the first floor.

WILLIAM PATTERSON – 1899

143.   *191 West Main Street*

In 1898, William H. Lewis arranged the sale of a parcel of land between his brother Thomas and his father-in-law William Patterson, a retired Connecticut farmer who was born in Forfarshire, Scotland, in 1835. Bill Patterson moved into his newly constructed home in 1899 with his wife Jane (Mercer) Patterson, who was also Scottish born. They spent the next decade together until Jane's death in 1909. Sometime after that, Patterson's daughter Bessie, who was by then divorced from William Lewis, moved into the house with her two sons Willard and Everett. Bessie (Patterson) Lewis remained in the house with her family, taking care of her father until his death in 1923. The house was left to her in her father's will and she and her son Everett remained there until 1950 ending 51 years of Patterson occupancy with the sale of the house to Constance Kuhl.

Looking east down West Main Street circa 1920.

Constance Kuhl owned the house for eleven years and during that time utilized it as an investment property, renting it out to numerous tenants. In 1961, she sold it to Lawyer John Kelaghan. It is not certain whether he also used this as a rental property or had a law office here. In 1963, it was purchased by Dr. Bruno Franek. German immigrant Bruno Franek was a highly respected psychiatrist who practiced primarily in East Greenwich but had an office here in Wickford for five years; he eventually focused his practice on substance and alcohol abuse and became the medical director at Edgehill Newport. He eventually sold the house to Joseph Morrissey, who resold it to Stanford Cashdollar in 1969.

Dr. Stan Cashdollar was a University of Rhode Island professor who taught the Classics – Latin, Greek, Classic Literature and the like. He eventually rose to the head of the language department at the University and, working with a URI volcanologist, published numerous scholarly works on Pompeii and Mt. Vesuvius. Dr. Cashdollar and his family lived here for 15 years selling the house to Roland Gervais in 1984. Later owners include the Niles, Daugherty, Tellier, and Carcone families.

George S. Holloway – circa 1850

144.   *8205 Post Road*

This unassuming house was constructed around 1850 for farmer George S. Holloway and his wife Lydia; as the Holloway family was populated with ship and house carpenters, it is likely that it was built by one of George's relations. George had purchased the lot in 1848 from his sister Susan E. Holloway and his brother William Holloway Jr. The house lot had been carved out of the Holloway's "corner orchard" prior to its sale to George. In all US census surveys George Holloway lists himself as a farmer or gardener and it would seem that he tended to the various farmlands owned by the Holloway family in the area. George and Lydia lived here the remainder of their lives and upon George's death in 1898, the house was purchased by Ebenezer "Eben" Brown.

Mercy (Brown) Vaughn

Ebenezer Brown was a retired and widowed farmer who moved here with his unmarried daughter Sarah Frances Brown after turning his farm over to his son. In 1905, Eben Brown sold the property to another daughter, Mercy (Brown) Vaughn who lived in Frenchtown. He included a caveat in the bill of sale that he was to be allowed to live out his life in the house. Ebenezer died there in 1918, and his daughters sold the house to Charles E. Webster in 1922.

Charles Webster, like Ebenezer Brown, was a retired farmer and he moved into the house with his wife Harriet

Charles Ernest Webster standing in front of his home circa 1930.

(Congdon) from their farm located in the Briggs Corner section of East Greenwich near the intersections of South Road and the South County Trail. Harriet Webster passed away ten years later and in 1934 Charles, who served as a deacon at the Frenchtown Baptist Church, remarried, this time to Harriet Huling. Just prior to Charles' death in 1942, the house was sold to Mildred "Millie" Hood, when he relocated to nearby Exeter.

Mildred Hood

The well-loved, but never married, Millie Hood worked for 43 years at the Narragansett Electric Company local office on Brown Street in the village. In addition to her kind spirit and good nature, her "claim to fame" locally, rested on the fact that her brother Ralph B. Hood was the founder, president and CEO of Velcro USA, the man instrumental in bringing the ubiquitous product Velcro from Switzerland where it was invented to not only America but the world in general. Ralph Hood, who held the US patent rights to Velcro, immediately saw the potential in it when he secured those rights in 1952, and you can

be sure that this house was home to some of Velcro's earliest adaptations. Millie stayed here in this house until her eventual retirement from Narragansett Electric in 1973. She then moved to Weare, New Hampshire, to a home owned by her brother Ralph, who ran his business out of nearby Manchester. Millie sold her home to local attorney, Leo Sullivan.

Leo Sullivan eventually transformed this small home into law office space, a function it held for decades until just recently when it was remodeled for use as a real estate office by V. N. Fraioli, and then a dog grooming and pet daycare facility.

THE ANDREWS/EMERY HOUSE – 1910

145.   *8225 Post Road*

C lamcakes as big as baseballs! The best blueberry pie this side of Mother
Prentice herself! Gazing at the unassuming little shed-like building in
the accompanying photo, these are probably not the phrases that would
come to mind to the average motorist sitting at the light at the top of West Main
Street waiting to turn into "Ye Olde Quaint & Historic." But long-time residents
of North Kingstown know differently. You see, from 1936 to 1969 this little building was the home of Waldo and Carmen (Andrews) Emery's Clamcake shack,
and its opening each year was "sure as shootin'" a sign of the beginning of the
summer season.

Folks would stand in line, eager to pull up a stool at the window and order up
a batch of those wonderful hot clamcakes or bite into a slab of Carmen's famous
pie made fresh each day in the house just above the shack. You've got to use your
imagination a bit to envision how it was back then. First and most importantly,
Post Road was only one lane in each direction and the intersection with West
Main was certainly much less imposing and a bit more pedestrian friendly than it
is today. Wickfordites and Lafayetteer's alike would happily "hoof it" from their
homes to Emery's for a bite of their favorite pie or a slightly greasy brown bag
of those wonderful clamcakes. Others, not lucky enough to be within walking
distance, would hop in the family jalopy, or hitch a ride to make the pilgrimage.
Waldo, who worked as a chauffeur in the off-season, would be there each day

The Emery's Clam Shack circa 1940s.

holding court and dispensing both clamcakes and camaraderie. A number of local youths got their first taste of the working world behind the counter helping out during those busy summer nights. Summer truly ended when those doors would swing closed for the season each Fall.

This house, built by Doctor Alexander MacDonald of Wickford in 1910 and known by locals as the "Doc MacDonald Cottage" came into the family through Carmen's father Alonzo Andrews, who bought it as a retirement home from Doc MacDonald in 1919. His daughter and new son-in-law moved in too, and the house was left to Carmen when Alonzo died in September of 1921. After 55 years of ownership, Waldo and Carmen sold the place in 1974 and relocated to San Marcos, Texas, to be near their son William's family. Since 1974, the Emery place has been used as a multi-family rental property, and fewer and fewer folks remember that great pie and those enormous clamcakes.

Carmen (Andrews) and Waldo Emery

I'll be the first to admit that there have been, and still are, plenty of places to get great clamcakes here in North Kingstown since Waldo and Carmen closed Emery's for the final season way back in 1969. But few of them have ever been held so dearly in the collective memory of "Our Fair Town." It's a pleasure to me that the old shack is still there to remind us of what was one a simpler time.

Thomas G. Lawton – 1887

146.   *37 Standpipe Lane*

Tuesday, November 22, 1892, was a dark day for the greater Lawton clan spread out across North Kingstown and Exeter. Tragic, but not wholly unexpected, news spread from one Lawton relation to the next.

Tom Lawton, you see, had finally given in to the demons that had possessed him. He walked out of his home, the one he generously shared with an elderly and otherwise homeless acquaintance, Desire Himes, carrying a large Colt revolver. He headed down the drive to a large rock in front of this fine home on Old Baptist Road he had recently constructed, gun in hand. Carefully and deliberately he placed it just above his left ear and then, without hesitation, he pulled the trigger. All Desire Himes, who was home at the time, could do was stand there in horror and watch the scene unfold. It happened that fast; Lawton was that sure of his plan of action—no one could stop him.

Tom Lawton was lost and overwhelmed in a struggle with crushing debt and the effects of an alcohol problem that began with attempts to drown his troubles with drink. On that November day in 1892, it appears that the 46-year-old had had enough. He ended his rollercoaster life the only way he could in that time before modern psychiatry.

Lawton left behind a legacy of sorts, though. You see, when he was in his right mind, he was an extraordinarily talented homebuilder. Although he constructed numerous fine homes, including the Meadowlands Bed and Breakfast house on

The house Thomas G. Lawton built on Old Baptist Road.

Old Baptist Road where he perished, and the fine house of H. Irving Reynolds on Pleasant Street, his piece-de-resistance, perhaps, is the Standpipe lane House build by Lawton in 1887.

Lawton still owned the Standpipe Lane house at the time of his demise on that sad afternoon in 1892. It was sold at auction early in 1893 and purchased by recently retired Providence jewelry craftsman Ames Hobart and his son, a trained machinist also working in Providence, Francis Hobart.

The Hobarts owned the house until 1914, when Francis got a new career in the Detroit area designing torpedoes for the "Great War." The Hobarts sold the home in 1914 to a recent English immigrant, Ernest Cheetham, who was also a homebuilder and general contractor. Cheetham is most well remembered by NK old-timers for what he and then his son, Ernest, Jr., did after he "retired" from the home building trade. From 1950 until the 1980s the Cheethams ran a secondhand furniture store at the old boarding house building in nearby Lafayette. Many a new family or a Navy clan passing through town bought and sold their furniture at the Cheetham place on Ten Rod Road.

The Cheethams owned the home for 54 years and were generous enough to sell the back portion of the property to the town in 1938 for a site for the emergency construction of a water tower after the crisis brought about by the 1938 hurricane. The Cheetham's long driveway off of Post Road eventually became Standpipe Lane. They sold their home in 1968 to the Peet family, who own it now in its 120th year.

I'm sure Tom Lawton, free from the torment that ended his days, is immensely pleased when he looks upon the fine home that stands as a monument to his ability and craft. Rest easy Tom Lawton, rest easy.

THE FRANKLIN HOUSE INN – CIRCA 1785

147.   *1 Tower Hill Road*

This double chimney-stacked two and one half story Federal style inn, with extensive Victorian-era remodeling, was originally constructed around 1785 by John and Hannah (Boone) Franklin on the site of the home of Hannah's parents, Samuel Boone Jr. and Mary (Wightman) Boone. The Boone family had been literally rent asunder by the consequences of the Revolutionary War, with Sam Boone Jr. and his adult son William refusing to join the rebels and his three adult daughters Hannah (married to Franklin), Anna (married to Nicholas Spink), and Mary (married to William Gardiner) following their husband's lead in asserting their intentions to support the Revolution at all costs. Those costs included the breakup of this family; with Samuel, his wife Mary, and William leaving Wickford, considered as traitorous Tory Loyalists, and the daughters staying behind in Wickford with their families. Sam Jr. and his group ended up in British held territory on Long Island and settled at what was then known as George's Manor and assisted in the construction of the British fortifications there, known as Fort St. George. In the Fall of 1780, according to a British report of the incident, "A party of rebels, about eighty in number, headed, it is said, by a rebel, Major Talmadge, assisted by a certain Heatheast, Muirson, Benjah Strong, Thomas Jackson and Caleb Brewster, officers belonging to said party, all formerly of Long Island, came across in eight whale-boats, etc., just after daylight arrived at Smith's Point, St. George's Manor, south side Long Island, where they surprised a respectable body of refugees belonging to Rhode Island and the vicinity, who were establishing a post in order to get a subsistence for themselves and families, etc." Samuel Boone Jr., and perhaps his wife Mary, were captured in this raid with William escaping and making his way to Canada. Samuel Boone Jr. was eventually transferred to a prisoner of war camp, Camp Security in Lancaster, Pennsylvania, where he later perished sometime in 1781. Mary, who somehow made it back to Wickford, died in September of 1782 and was buried in the Boone graveyard, just south of the Phillips Street-Tower Hill Road intersection. Her gravestone not only notes the particulars of her death, but also mentions Samuel's demise in Lancaster. In an interesting side note, William Boone, in July of 1800, in absentia, contested the ownership of this property. He himself, still considered a traitor to the United States of America, was not allowed entry into Rhode Island to attend the legal proceedings, and instead sent his Canadian born son and attorney Henry Boone to represent him in the legal proceedings. Out of "affection for their brother" the three sisters consented to pay William a sum of money for his share of their parent's estate.

William Boone, forever banned from entering the United States for his Loyalist leanings, is buried in Burtts Corner, New Brunswick where he and many other loyal British subjects resettled after the Revolution.

When the widower John Franklin, son of Abel Franklin of Jamestown, married Hannah she too was widowed, as her first husband, Joseph Clarke, who she had married in 1762, died in June of 1770. John and Hannah built this inn, on the site of her parent's house, to take advantage of the traffic on the busy Boston Post Road, the main thoroughfare between Boston and New York City at that time. Its location at the entrance to Wickford also helped to keep this regular stagecoach stop busy on a year round basis. Records also indicate that the North Kingstown Town Council met here frequently as well. John Franklin died in August of 1806, leaving Hannah a widow once again. To help her out with the inn, her aunt, Hannah (Boone) Coggeshall, widow of Daniel Coggeshall and sister of Wightman Boone, moved in permanently at the Franklin Inn. In 1829, these two widowed women, who were of similar age, legalize the arrangement in which they run the Inn, when Hannah Franklin sells one half share of the property to Hannah Coggeshall. In 1832, apparently in failing health, Hannah Franklin sold her half share to Hannah Coggeshall retaining a life estate in the property allowing her to live out her days there. In 1835, Hannah Franklin must have passed away, as at that time Hannah Coggeshall sold the Inn to Nicholas Fry, whose mother was a member of the Coggeshall family.

Nicholas and Esther Fry of East Greenwich ran the Franklin House as an Inn for a time and then leased the building to Jonathan Slocum who operated it as a boarding house. At the same time, the Frys sold the surrounding acreage to the Holloway family who established a peach and apple orchard on the 20 acre parcel. In 1846 the Frys sold the house itself to Mary Holloway, who reunited it with the farmlands the family had purchased earlier. In 1858, the Holloways sold the entire parcel, including "the dwelling house, barn, corn crib, and orchards to Anthony and Clarissa Turner.

Well known and successful farmer Anthony Turner, lived here with his family and worked the land from 1858 until 1866. At that time he sold this farm and moved south down the Post Road a short ways and purchased the larger farm parcel that is now the site of the new St. Bernard's Catholic Church. The Franklin House's new owner was merchant and farmer Thomas B. Vaughan. Sadly, Thomas and Almira Vaughan's time here at the Franklin House was short. He suffered a massive stroke and died at the age of 56 in 1869. The house was purchased from his widow by his brother, prominent manufacturer Syria Vaughan shortly after his death. Syria, who lived on West Main Street, owned the house for only a short, most likely to allow his widowed sister-in-law time to get her affairs in order, and sold it in 1873 to wealthy Providence manufacturer William R. Talbot and his wife Mary Cornelia (Arnold) Talbot.

Now the Talbots were Providence folks. They lived on Williams Street in that city in a home famous thereabouts for its "Gaspee Room," a room removed intact from a family home on South Main Street in which the plan for the destruction of the British ship *Gaspee* was formulated. William Talbot traced his ancestry back to Major Silas Talbot, a hero of the Revolutionary War. His wife, Mary, could trace hers back to Welcome Arnold, one of the financiers of the Colonial Army as well as Captain Barnes McKay, an officer under General George Washington. Mr. Talbot owned and operated the Tockwotten Button Company in Providence where he manufactured buttons and upholstery nails for RI's burgeoning fabric industry and was part owner of a number of other textile industry related concerns. He was quite successful at this enterprise and the family was very well off. Each summer they would move their household down from Providence and stay at the Franklin House, which they renamed Barberry Hill. It was the Talbot family who extensively remodeled the house, adding numerous Victorian era embellishments including the charming widow's walk, the large front parlor windows looking out upon the graceful sitting porch, and the detailed trim. The rubble stone foundation was also faced at this time in brick, and the federal period chimneys were rebuilt into the detailed Victorian replacements extant today. Eventually the entire area, which had for decades been known as Franklin's Corner became identified by all as Talbot's Corner to honor one of Wickford's most popular and consistent summer families. The Talbots had four children; one son and three daughters. Eventually one daughter, Helen, married J. Benton

Porter of Philadelphia, and the Porters, as well, would come along. I imagine those summers as being idyllic and consisting of teas and picnics by the seashore. As the 1800s turned into the 1900s, the elder Talbots joined their Revolutionary ancestors in heaven and the home passed down to the three daughters, known in Wickford simply as the Talbot sisters. The Talbot sisters were quite religious and proud of their heritage. They were involved in the DAR both here and in Providence, and were known to have hand woven many vestments for local churches including St. Paul's in Wickford where they attended. The Talbot sisters continued to summer in Wickford right to the bitter end when Helen, the last of them, passed away quietly in her sleep at her beloved Barberry Hill. Her widower, J. Benton Porter, in 1947 sold off the summer house and its 45 acres and returned to Philadelphia.

The next owner of the house was real estate agent Rosalind Wallace, who quickly sub-divided the extensive Talbot/Porter real estate holdings and sold the old inn, with only a minimal amount of land, to Clarence and Zella Signor who retooled the now ancient building into an apartment house. Since that time it has been owned by the Ashworth, Burum, Ferdinanelli, Quinn, Wescott, Dworman, Noonan, and DiSaia families; all of whom have operated it as an apartment house. It was purchased by its present owner Christopher Squillante in 2001. Chris has done extensive restoration to the old Franklin House and maintains it in a fashion that surely please even the Talbot clan.

This 1945 aerial photograph shows the extensive farmfields and the many outbuildings associated with the Talbot's agricultural enterprises.

Talbot Estate Caretaker House – circa 1880

148.   **35 Tower Hill Road**

This house, also known as the "Boss Farmer's House," was caused to be constructed around 1880 by William R. Talbot to be utilized as the housing for the caretaker for the numerous Talbot properties in the immediate vicinity. Not only was the caretaker responsible for the upkeep of all the Talbot family houses and rental properties, he was also expected to have the capabilities necessary to take care of the extensive grounds and the small hobby farm that the Talbots maintained. The earliest "Boss Farmers" known to have lived and worked here were William Havens and then Thomas Baker who held the position in the late 1800s. They were followed by Alfred A. Sherman, who lived here with his wife Lorena (Congdon) and their children and served as the property caretaker from around the beginning of the 1900s until around 1915. In 1915, the Boss Farmer position was assumed by Clifford Arnold who moved into the house with his wife Minnie (Hayes). Clifford took care of all the houses and buildings at Talbot's corner for the remainder of the time that they owned the property, some forty years. The Talbots and Porters were so fond of their 'Boss Farmer' that at the time of the final sale of the Talbot Estate in 1947, they carved off a small house lot fronting on Standpipe Lane and gifted it to Clifford and Minnie. This house, along with the main house was sold as one parcel to real estate agent Rosalind Wallace in June of 1947. Wallace sub-divided the larger parcel and sold the Caretaker house to Winston W. Stadig Sr. in December of that year.

Winston Stadig moved in here with his wife Charlotte (St. Germain) and children at the start of 1948. Prior to this time, he was a mold maker in the jewelry industry with a background and degree in sculpture from the Rhode Island School of Design. He worked as real estate agent for a time, working in fact for Rosalind Wallace, and then in 1950, took a civilian position at the Davisville Naval Construction Battalion Center, where he worked as the editor and principal writer of bi-weekly base newspaper, "The Yardarm." He held this position until his retirement in 1971. In his free time, Winston Stadig enjoyed sculpting, working in both brass and clay. Stadig was quite well known in his time for the creation of six inch high caricature sculptures of famous people of the day. His numerous subjects included the likes of RI Governor T. F. Green, Presidents Taft, Roosevelt, and Truman, foreign dignitaries such as Stalin and Churchill and popular entertainers such as W. C. Fields. Stadig often sent copies of these statuettes to their subjects and indeed sent a full set of Yalta Conference attendees, Churchill, Stalin, and Roosevelt, to President Roosevelt himself. These statues, designed and created by Winston Stadig are on display at the Roosevelt Museum at Hyde Park. Winston Stadig Sr. died in June of 1986; the house is still owned and occupied by his son Winston Stadig Jr.

Winston Stadig's caricature sculptures.

THE GEORGE THOMAS STORE/ KATYDID
COTTAGE TEA ROOM BUILDING – 1856

149.   *30 Tower Hill Road*

Sometimes, the most innocuous of buildings can have the most intriguing of histories. Such is definitely the case with the unassuming apartment building that sits placidly at 30 Tower Hill Road. It's fair to say that we've all glanced at it as we've sat impatiently waiting for the light at West Main to change. To look at it you'd probably never guess she's even as old as she is, no less imagine the interesting events which have played out under her eaves.

The core of this building was constructed in 1856 by George P. Thomas on land he had purchased from Jonathan and Susan Slocum. George Thomas constructed a general store here and operated out of this location for nearly a decade. Around 1864, he decided to relocate his business into Wickford Village proper and, in partnership with his new son-in-law C. Allen Chadsey, opened a larger store on Brown Street. George Thomas sold his old storefront to Providence hotel keeper Nathaniel Stearns and his brother Francis in April of 1866.

Nathaniel Stearns and his family ran the Adams Hotel in Providence, a busy hotel/boarding house that catered to not only transient visitors to the capital city but also a large number of regular boarders who worked in the city's numerous factories. His brother Francis was a soap merchant who sold soap commercially to the textile and laundry industries in the region. Nathaniel remodeled the Thomas Store into a getaway cottage for his family, and Francis constructed another small cottage on the same parcel for his. They used these cottages to get away from the heat, pollution, hustle and bustle of Rhode Island's industrialized urban core whenever they could. They both passed away, by the middle of the 1870s and their families sold the parcel to William and Cornelia Talbot, who also had, albeit on a much grander scale, a getaway home here at the intersection of West Main Street and Tower Hill Road.

This building's story then restarts, in a way, when it was remade around 1877. I say in a way, because the gentleman who constructed her actually made her out of three smaller structures. William Talbot, the man for whom this area of town, Talbot's Corner, was named, took the two small cottages, which were on this lot facing his big summer home across the street, and combined them with a small abandoned "Holy Rollers" Meeting House (to quote his daughter, Helen Talbot Porter) which he moved from somewhere on Ten Rod Road (most likely the Exeter Advent Christian Church, once located just over the line in Exeter) to the lot and made the building that we see today. So, although the house was "put together" in 1877, parts of it are actually somewhat older.

Little is known of the building's history until around the turn of the century, when Talbot rented it out to Mrs. Lucille Luth. Mrs. Luth joined the latest craze that was sweeping the area at that time, and opened up a tea room on the street level of the building. Her tea room, unlike many others of that era, was an un-qualified success due to Mrs. Luth's abilities as a cook. It quickly became a main-stay on Talbot's Corner and can be seen in the accompanying photograph. It is curious to note that, on the telephone pole right next to the tea room is a sign for one of Mrs. Luth's main competitors, Mother Prentice's Wickford House. The Luth family operated the Katydid Cottage until the early 1930s when she abandoned this location and opened a new tea room on Fowler Street down in Wickford proper. Again her reputation as a great cook held her in good stead, as a few long-time residents of the village can still remember the crowds that flocked to her establishment. It has been said that it was the favorite lunch stop for the RI

State Police, who at that time, had their barracks at 24 Brown Street right in the heart of the village, sort of the historic predecessor to the ubiquitous donut shop of the present day.

Back up at Talbot's Corner, the old Katydid Cottage was being treated in the same manner as all empty buildings were at that time. She was being carved up into apartments to take advantage of the opportunities presented by the virtual tidal wave of folks coming into North Kingstown to construct and later serve at Quonset/Davisville. During the first half of the 1940s, the building was rented by Earl North Sr. and his wife Bertha (Tingley) North. They ran the building as a boarding house of sorts, and had as their tenants, a whole cadre of carpenters and tradesmen bought to the village by the US Navy to build the Wickford Housing Project across West Main Street in what is now Wilson Park. The North family kept in contact with some of these men for many years. She would fade from the historic record right then and there if it wasn't for the fact that shortly after the close of WWII, a young jug-eared Texan bound for eventual fame and fortune rented an apartment in the building for himself and his new wife while he trained at the base. To paraphrase that now famous character, "It's tales like this that make you want to pop the hood on this baby's history, stick your head in there and see what makes her tick." This swamp Yankee wonders what Mr. and Mrs. Ross Perot would think of their old apartment now.

Ross Perot

The Talbot clan sold the house in 1945 to Roland B. Wood, the first of a long string of landlords that have owned it since its Talbot days. These include Nathaniel Hendrick, Craig Randall, Robert Motherway, Stephen Heard and Gordon Young. Since the year 2000 it has been owned by Christopher Squillante who has spiffed it up quite a bit. Perhaps old Ross Perot may stop by some day and take a look-see.

NICHOLAS SPINK – CIRCA 1774

150.   *264 West Main Street*

Assigning a construction date to this interesting little cape style home is difficult due to the condition of North Kingstown's early real estate records, the property's late 18th and early 19th century history as a small portion of a much larger Spink owned parcel, and the fact that it was extensively remodeled by 20th century owners. It most certainly shows up in an 1807 document in which Samuel Spink transfers his share of the ownership of the "house with the basement room" to his brothers Boone and Christopher Spink, and the 1839 real estate transaction through which Christopher's widow Hannah sells it to Arnold W. Congdon. Nicholas Spink, who was nearly an "empty-nester" when he constructed his new home and hatmaker's shop just to the east of here in 1796, most certainly raised his family in a home here on this larger Spink parcel and the language of the 1807 document infers that this house with its basement room was that colonial-era home. A detailed analysis of the house's remaining original structural timbers and chimney stack configuration, which is not possible at this time due to access issues, would go a long way towards resolving this mystery. At this time, based upon the information I have, I have assigned it a date that coincides with the birth of Nicholas and Hannah (Boone) Spink's first child. No information is available about how the house was used between 1796 and its sale to Arnold Congdon some 43 years later. Most likely it spent time as both a Spink family member home and as a rental property. Whatever the circumstances were, it is certain that in 1839, Arnold and Lydia Congdon moved into the home.

Arnold W. Congdon and his wife Lydia both began their lives together as husband and wife after emerging from personal tragedy. Arnold's first wife, Mercy Ann (Rathbun), died in childbirth at the age of 24 while giving birth to Arnold Jr., who died just one month later. Lydia's (Peirce) first husband, Isaac Spink died suddenly at the age of 25 leaving her with two sons. Arnold, formerly of Swamptown, and Lydia, who had lived in Shermantown, purchased this house from Hannah Spink, who was a distant relation to Lydia's deceased first husband, and moved here with her sons Eugene and Isaac Jr. In 1859 they had a son together, who they named Samuel after Lydia's father Samuel W. Peirce. Arnold spent his life working as a farm laborer and his two stepsons Eugene and Isaac Spink worked as fishermen out of Wickford Harbor as soon as they were able. Arnold and Lydia owned this home until 1865 and after that rented space from another relation of Lydia's first husband, Samuel Spink (known as "Wooden Leg Sammy" to differentiate him from the many other Sam Spink's that were living in North Kingstown at that time) out at the Spink farm on Newcomb Road before moving eventually to South Coventry, Connecticut. Lydia died there on Christmas Day in 1873 and was brought back to Shermantown and buried next to her first husband Isaac in the Spink family graveyard there. Arnold died five years later and was buried back in Swamptown next to Mercy Ann and their infant son in the Rathbun graveyard.

The next owners of this house were Rufus and Susan C. (Northup) Rose, who purchased it in 1865 from the Congdons. Rufus was a local stone mason who worked with relation William Rose, of Rose Hill in Saunderstown, in the stone mason's trade. Rufus and Susan moved in with their adult son Benjamin Rose, who worked as a laborer with his father, and daughters Susan, who worked in a nearby textile mill, and Elizabeth, who was still in school. A decade or so later, little had changed other than Elizabeth had gotten married to local lad Thomas A. Baker, who was working as the boss farmer/caretaker of the nearby Talbot estate and was living here in the home. Around 1880, when the Talbots constructed the caretaker's cottage (see 35 Tower Hill Road), Thomas and Elizabeth moved out of this house and took up residence on the Talbot estate itself. Rufus died in 1886 at the age of 72. At that time Susan transferred owner-

Rufus M. Rose

ship of this house to her other adult son John Browning Rose who was a grocer, with a life estate allowing her to live out her days there. Unfortunately John Rose ended up in financial difficulties and lost this house to the Wickford Savings Bank in 1899. The Rose family relocated to Richmond, RI, after this sad turn of events and the house was purchased from the bank by the Talbot family and folded into their extensive real estate holdings at this intersection, which was by then known as "Talbot's Corner."

The Talbots used this house, like so many other nearby properties, as an income producing rental property while they owned it. The Boss Farmer/caretaker was responsible for rent collection and maintenance of these rental properties for the Talbot/Porter clan, who lived in Providence when not summering here in Wickford. It stayed in the ownership of this family until the eventual breakup of the Talbot's family holdings in 1947; at that time it was purchased by Nathaniel and Helen Hendrick.

Nathaniel Hendrick was a local businessman who had very diversified interests. He was a real estate developer, real estate sales agent and appraiser, a

Nathaniel Hendrick

landlord with extensive rental holdings, a well respected local auctioneer, and operator of a home heating oil delivery business. He remodeled this building, into rental units upstairs and set up his home heating oil business office in what the Spink clan had called the 'basement room" with its entry door right on the side of West Main Street. He was an active member of the local Masonic Lodge as well. Nathaniel Hendrick died two days before the 1954 hurricane hit Wickford; this building stayed in Hendrick family ownership until 1972. Later owners, which included the Randall, Conaboy, House, and D'Ambra families, have maintained it as a rental property. It is now owned and cared for by John Russo who lives in this ancient little home.

THADDEUS HUNT – 1887

151.   *250 West Main Street*

This house was constructed in 1887 by local house carpenter Daniel Lawton for Thaddeus and Laura (Chase) Hunt and their son William. The Hunts had purchased two lots the year previous, one from Daniel Lawton and one from Alfred Eldred, and had combined them for the construction of their new home. They called their stately home "Hillside." The land itself had a somber history connected to it as it was former location of the Wickford winter crypt, constructed by village resident William Brown and utilized by villagers as a temporary "resting place" for the dearly departed who passed away during the winter months when the ground was frozen too hard for grave digging. With the opening of the Elm Grove Cemetery winter crypt in the 1850s this crypt was no longer needed, but the land, known by all as the "tomb lot" sat understandably empty for many decades.

Thaddeus Hunt, who had grown up in the village attending the Wickford Academy and then Eastman Business College in Poughkeepsie, NY, had spent seventeen years after graduating from college working as a clerk and bookkeeper for Allen Mason Thomas at his store A. M. Thomas & Son Dry Goods. In 1883, he was hired as the head cashier at the Wickford National Bank, a position he held for quite some time until he became manager of the bank after it was absorbed by the Industrial Trust Bank.

Thaddeus Hunt

Hillside, the home of Laura and Thaddeus Hunt, circa 1910.

He held that position for 30 more years, spending a total of 51 years working in the same bank building. He also served 27 years on the Town School committee and 14 years as the town's auditor. On top of all this, Thaddeus Hunt was also President of the Library board of trustees and for 40 years served as superintendent of the Wickford Baptist Church Sunday School. His wife Laura Chase was born on Nantucket, daughter of mariner William Chase. Her mother Elizabeth (Congdon) Chase had familial roots that extended back to the Congdons of Wickford. Thaddeus died in the house in 1934 and Laura in 1936. She left the home to her granddaughters Marguerite and Dorothy Hunt, who rented it out to Wickford physician Albert C. Henry. In 1941, they sold Hillside to Dr. Henry and his wife Doris, who was a trained nurse.

Albert C. Henry was born in Bethlehem, Pennsylvania, and earned his medical degree in Allentown and Philadelphia. Soon after graduation from Hahnemann Medical College in Philadelphia he came to Wickford and began to practice medicine. Besides his private practice, he served as the NK School Dept. physician, was president of the medical staff at South County Hospital and was accepted as a member of the staff at Roger Williams Hospital. His wife Doris worked with him in his practice, which they ran out of the house, and served as the school nurse. An avid golfer, he was one of the founders of the Annaquatucket Country Club, which was located at the present day site of the NK High School, and was a member of the Winnapaug Country Club in Westerly. He was stricken with a fatal heart attack on the 13th fairway at Winnapaug in August of 1956 and died without being revived. His wife and family stayed in the house until 1961, when they sold it to George LaPorte.

George LaPorte opened a dental practice in the offices once occupied by Dr. Henry. He operated here for many years and then the house was sold to chiropractor Vincent Brunnelle and his wife April in 1997. They continue a tradition of more than 80 years of medical or dental care being dispensed from the grand home of Thaddeus Hunt.

Harry Hargreaves – 1906

152.   *210 West Main Street*

This fine home was built in 1906 for English immigrants Harry and Helen B. Hargreaves. Harry Hargreaves was an experienced textile worker who listed himself on all official documents as a dyer or dye house foreman. He lived here in the house for only a short time and was most likely employed at either the Gregory Mill in Wickford or the Rodman Mill in nearby Lafayette. In 1910 he sold the house and moved to East Providence where he worked in the same occupation; a decade later he is again working at a textile mill in North Attleboro, Massachusetts, where he and Helen finished their lives. The Hargreaves sold this home to Charles C. and Hattie A. Pierce.

In December of 1910 when Charles purchased this house, he was a motorman working for the Sea View Electric Trolley Line which ran through the village on its way from East Greenwich to the Narragansett Pier. He sold the house in 1919 to take a job with as a railroad overseer on the main line working out of Slocum. He later worked for a state highway crew and then spent a few years working for the Rodman Manufacturing Company. After retiring from the Rodman mill in 1948, he started Pierce's Turkey Farm on Tower Hill Road, a business which ran well into the late 20th century, with his son Charles C. Pierce Jr. Charles and Hattie Pierce sold this home, in August of 1919, to a Sea View Line co-worker Matthew W. Clarke and his wife Elizabeth.

Matthew W. Clarke was also a motorman, or driver, for the Sea View Electric Trolley line for many years and was locally renowned for the fact that he drove not only the first but also the last trolley car that ran the entire route from East Greenwich to Narragansett. The Sea View Line shut down just a short while after Clarke purchased this home, and he soon secured a position working for the State Board of Public Roads as a foreman in charge of the line- painting crews, a task that was done largely by hand in this timeframe. A year before his death in 1936, he lost that position and began a career as a painting contractor. He was working under contract to the town of North Kingstown, repainting the Town Hall interior when he died from pneumonia in 1936. His wife Elizabeth, and adult daughter Eleanor, who was a local high school English teacher, stayed in the house after Matthew's death, selling it in 1940 to local physician and surgeon Dr. Gordon Menzies.

Dr. Gordon Menzies

Dr. Gordon Menzies was a second generation physician who received his medical degree at Edinburgh University and did his residency at a hospital in Dublin. He served in the US Army during WWII as a Colonel in the North African theatre and bought this house for his family consisting of wife Lillian (Gale) and two sons Gordon and Bruce. After the war's end he returned to Wickford and opened up a family practice which he ran out of this house for decades. Concurrently Dr. Menzies was a member of the staff at South County Hospital for 38 years. Gordon Menzies passed away in 1978 and his wife and sons continued to live in the home. Brothers Gordon and Bruce Menzies still live in the house to this day, extending Menzies ownership for more than 70 years.

LUKE J. WARD – 1911

153.   *196 West Main Street*

This house was constructed in 1911 on land owned by Peter Byrnes. The house was built for Peter's wife's nephew Luke Ward, whom they had adopted as a child, and his new wife Alice E. (McElhaney) Ward. Not long after moving in Luke and Alice had two children, John and Mary.

Luke Ward was born in 1884 in Bridgeport, Connecticut, the son of Christopher and Ann Ward. Christopher Ward was an Irish immigrant who had come to America to work in the textile industry, an industry in which he was a trained tradesman and in high demand. Sadly, not long after Luke had passed from boyhood to youth, both Christopher and Annie succumbed to one of the countless maladies that swept periodically through the closely settled factory towns of the day, and young Luke was an orphan with what might seem to be a dim future. Luck and the good Lord shined down upon Luke though, as word got to his uncle and aunt, Peter and Mary Byrnes, and before you knew it nine year old orphan child Luke Ward was on his way to Wickford, RI, and an adoption by Peter and Mary Byrnes of West Main Street. Luke held onto his last name in memory of his parents, but in every other way he was a part of the Byrnes family, eventually becoming an integral part of the family business, Peter Byrnes' Greenhouse and Flower Shop, right next door to the big Byrnes family home on West Main Street. Luke received his entire education within the public school system of North Kingstown and by the time he graduated in 1905, he was the well-liked and respected president of the very first class to graduate from North Kingstown's

Luke Ward, center, was the president of the first graduating class from the new North Kingstown High School in 1905.

new high school. He was also somewhat older at 20, than his classmates, as his life's circumstances had caused him to have a later start in his schooling. After graduation Luke went right back to work at the florist shop, although he did later attend Bryant College to learn the business ends of things. As a matter of fact, he listed his trade as florist on the marriage application he filled out when he married Alice McElhaney in 1908 and with the exception of a 12-year stint as postmaster of the Wickford Post Office from 1922 to 1934 (the post office was ironically in the same Gregory Building where most of his high school classes had been held), it was in that florist shop that he happily spent his days. Luke also loved the theatre; he was active in many local amateur theatre groups, and golf. Luke Ward was one of the founding members of the Annaquatucket Golf Club, the golf course which existed for decades on the site of the present day NK High School. Luke and Alice had two children, Mary and John. John Ward eventually became a newspaper man columnist and local historian. If any one person can be credited with much of what is in the South County Room at the town library, it is John Ward. Mary married Clarence Parker and stayed here in Wickford as well, operating the Wickford House on Main Street. Upon his mother's death in 1941, Luke and Alice moved into the larger Byrnes house next door and used this house as a rental property. It remained a Ward family owned rental property until 1973 when it was sold to David Burnham.

Local contractor Dave Burnham owned the house until 1976 when he sold it to Jon Verplank. The Verplanks owned it from 1976 until 1985 when they sold it to Peter Sabo. It was purchased by its present owner Stephanie Stevens from the Sabo family in 1993.

JOHN WARD – 1938

154.   *190 West Main Street.*

No doubt about it, this house is far from old by Wickford standards. In most cases, I wouldn't even include a home of this young age in such a tome. But this house is special; this was John Ward's house. You see, John Ward was a fixture in my life; he was one of my grandfather's closest friends and Mr. and Mrs. Ward populate my past as they do for so many other people who have lived in this village all their lives. If you could select an archetype for the "cantankerous but loveable old Swamp Yankee," John Ward would be your man. If there was ever a stereotypical newspaperman, pencil and pad in his pocket, plunking away at a reliable old manual typewriter, scouting out leads, searching for the perfect word or phrase that captures the nuances of his story, well John Ward's your guy again. No doubt about it, John Ward, like my grandfather, was one of my childhood heroes.

John Ward was born next door to this little West Main Street cottage, which was in turn situated right next door to his father's florist shop, in September of 1911. He went to school in town, and almost immediately after graduation was hired by the Providence Journal Bulletin as the staff reporter covering North Kingstown, Exeter, and Jamestown. Expected to be on the clock, on call at all times, he was paid a salary of $22.00 a week. He worked as a newspaperman for the rest of his life, ending his career, more than four decades later as a staff writer for the Sunday Journal magazine, the *Rhode Islander*. While journalism was his vocation, local history was his avocation, a passion he wore like a comfortable

sweater. John Ward was the prime force; the driving wheel behind the success of the South County Museum founded here in North Kingstown and later relocated to Narragansett. He was an active member of the Gilbert Stuart's Birthplace group and was a board member of the RI Historical Society. John Ward was a tireless advocate for the NK Free Library's South County Room and donated so much ephemera, photographs, and memorabilia that they started a John Ward collection just to keep track of it all. John Ward was also passionate about the history of firefighting here in South County and was instrumental in the retention and restoration of the town's old handpumper Washington #1. John Ward, like so many of his era, also loved railroads, and he worked tirelessly to document the history of railroading in the region. And oh yeah, he was a founder of the Wickford Lions Club, the NK Ambulance Association, and Babe Ruth baseball in the community. John Ward never stood on the sidelines waiting for something to get done. He stood up, stepped forward and made things happen. As you can imagine, this old swamp Yankee who was a hero in my childhood, kept that title in my mind as long as he lived. No "feet of clay" here, not John Ward. But as time has gone on I've come to the realization that he's more than a hero for me, he's a role model. You see John Ward was what I aspire today to be: the historian as a storyteller. His history lessons came alive through the way he told the tale. They were populated with folks just as unique as himself and situations that were made memorable by his ability to captivate an audience as spun his yarns. To honor John Ward and all that he stood for, I'm going to tell one right now....

Part of my childhood holiday tradition, whether it be Christmas, Thanksgiving, or the Fourth of July, in Wickford back in the 1960s was a process my parents called "making the rounds." We'd visit all the relatives and family friends, staying for a while at each place, snacking on this and that, talking with this one and that one, and then moving on to the next stop in "the rounds." Our day would always end at my mother's parents, the St. Pierre's on West Main Street, and on occasion, the stop at Grandma and Grandpa St. Pierre's would include a stroll

Mr. and Mrs. John Ward

across the street to Mr. and Mrs. Ward's house. For a time the Ward's ran a shop on Post Road called Bird Cage Candies, so me and my sister Julie, well heck we looked forward to a treat of broken ribbon candy or misshaped chocolates that Mrs. Ward would save for us. What a deal when you're a child, having the inside track with people who owned a candy store! Usually our visits at the Wards would proceed with all of the women and children heading off in one direction and Mr. Ward and my grandfather heading off in another. I understood, from overhearing my mother talking that Mr. Ward and Grandpa's visits occasionally included something called "Old Granddad," which confused me as a boy because I thought they were old granddads not sippers of "Old Granddad." Well anyway they would sit there, sometimes with their friend "Old Granddad," and laugh, eat chips and nuts and other holiday sort of treats, and talk grownup-men-talk about work and sports and whatever old stuff Mr. Ward was finding and whatever old stuff my grandfather was digging up. They shared this love of old stuff, although my grandfather truly seemed to feel that the best old stuff was stuff you dug up out of the earth and John Ward felt that the best old stuff was stuff you found in some old-timer's barn. They also shared a devilish streak, quite a sense of humor, and, unbeknownst to Julie and myself, a keen dislike of Mrs. Ward's cat. On one particular set of holiday rounds, Thanksgiving I believe, Mr. Ward and Grandpa must have got tired of talking about old stuff and cracking and eating fancy walnuts and communing with "Old Granddad" and turned their attentions and imagination upon Mrs. Ward's cat. It got awful quiet for a while in the living room where they were stationed in their usual easy chairs until all of a sudden there let go a racket like I have never heard before! Clickety-clacking, God-awful meowing and screeching, banging and careening, things falling everywhere, and above this deafening din rose the sound of two grown men, both in their fifties, laughing like little boys possessed. Their laughter rose like a chorus and filled the house. Remarkable! That is until Mrs. Ward's cat with its itty-bitty kitty feet jammed into walnut shells which were taped onto its paws careened into view in the hallway and sped clickity-clack out the front door!! Well then there was a whole different set of noises coming out of Mrs. Ward, my grandmother, and my mother centering around "grown men" and "set a good example" and the like. When I remarked to my mother later that night how interesting it was that messing with the cat got Mr. Ward and Grandpa both into the doghouse, she shushed me up quick, but not without letting a little smirk-like grin escape for just a second…

You know, if I close my eyes in the quietest part of the morning when I'm walking through Wickford and listen real hard, I swear I can almost hear John Ward calling out "Hello there Timmy-boy!" just like he used to all those years ago…. Hello to you too, John Ward and thanks a million.

Peter S. Byrnes – 1875/1906

155.   *180 West Main Street*

In November of 1905, florist and greenhouse operator Peter Byrnes purchased a parcel of land from Roy C. Nichols. This piece of land was once home to the popular summer hotel "The Elms," which in turn had once been a fine double house owned for many years by the Spink family. It had burned to the ground on Friday the 13th in January of that year, and when Byrnes purchased the lot, the only structure standing that had survived the intense blaze was a large circa 1875 barn/carriage house. Peter Byrnes had that barn converted into this large home, and constructed his florist shop and greenhouses upon the exact location where "The Elms" had previously stood.

Born in Ireland in 1857, Peter S. Byrnes came to this country as a child with his parents John and Jane Byrnes. He learned the florist trade as a young man and moved here to Wickford with his wife Mary (Ward) Byrnes to open his own shop. His innovative thinking and entrepreneurial spirit made him a success in this difficult business. He not only ran a full service florist shop here in Wickford, but for many years also operated a satellite store during the summer months at the Narragansett Pier. He would travel down to Narragansett each day in the summer, with his flowers in hand, on the Sea View Electric Trolley that ran through Wickford stopping on West Main Street near its present day intersection with Newtown Avenue. Peter also kept a large array of palms and large tropical plants in his greenhouses that he would rent out for use at weddings and parties. The entire Byrnes family, including their adopted nephew Luke Ward, worked alongside Peter running this

Peter Byrnes and his brother Patrick.

business. Indeed, upon Peter's retirement, Luke Ward took over the Byrnes Flowershop. Peter Byrnes was also very active in the Wickford fire department and served as Fire Chief for many years. Additionally he served as Commissioner of the Town Poor Farm for a time and also held a position as Town Sergeant. Peter Byrnes died in November of 1928 and is buried in Elm Grove Cemetery. His wife Mary continued to live in the house until her eventual death in 1941. Luke and Alice Ward then lived there until Luke's death in 1968. In 1970, his daughter Mary (Ward) Parker sold the house after 65 years of family ownership.

The house was purchased in 1970 by popular University of Rhode Island ornithologist and biology professor Frank Heppner. Heppner was known for his quirky teaching style that included appearances in Count Dracula regalia for a lecture on supernatural creatures and arrivals in his large lecture hall on a motorcycle. The house was sold by Heppner to its present owner Anthony Tietze in 1977.

View looking down West Main Street, showing Byrnes Greenhouse.

NICHOLAS SPINK – 1796

156.   **154 West Main Street**

T his house was constructed around 1796 for local hatter Nicholas Spink on a parcel of land he acquired from his father-in-law Samuel Boone. The house, most likely built by Nicholas and Hannah (Boone) Spink's son Daniel, included an attached hatmaker's shop, which has since been converted into living space. In April of 1807, an aging Nicholas Spink transferred ownership of the home to his son Samuel, also trained as a hatmaker, and his wife Barbara (Lindley), with a caveat attached to the deed detailing that he and Hannah be cared for in their old age. Samuel and Barbara evidently lived up to this task and in 1818, they sold the house and their share in countless other inherited properties which they owned in concert with Nicholas's brothers Boone, Christopher, and Daniel, to Christopher and Boone Spink and their wives. Samuel and Barbara Spink, along with their children Sarah Ann, Samuel Jr., Thomas L., Nicholas, and Charlotte, then moved to recently opened lands in Genesee County NY, joining a number of former North Kingstown residents already living there, in-cluding Spinks, Reynolds, and Browns, who had previously lived in Wickford. Nicholas Spink's home and hatshop stayed in the Spink family until 1837 when Christopher's widow, also named Hannah, sold it along with a large parcel of farmland to Jeremiah Greene Chadsey.

Jeremiah Greene Chadsey was born in December of 1780 to Jabez Chadsey Jr. and his wife Hannah (Greene), and was named after his maternal grandfather

Jeremiah Greene. Jeremiah Chadsey and his wife Avis (Wightman) came here from the Chadsey homestead farm off of what is now Chadsey Road, then part of the Boston Post Road. Although he began his time here in Wickford as a farmer, and a successful one at that, he was also an extraordinary entrepreneur who branched out and began new enterprises as opportunities presented themselves. Chadsey started by operating a grocery and dry goods store on Main Street in the village and then began a remarkable hand loom weaving industry through which he supplied 600 tabletop hand-looms to households in six different South County communities. Chadsey's arrangement with these 600 weavers, most of them women, was that they could use that loom free of charge to weave clothing for their families, as long as they wove a predetermined amount of cloth for him each month, and bought yarn from his Wickford store. Chadsey would periodically have this fabric picked up and would then sell it in his store as well. Additionally, these 600 weavers were also compensated for their efforts with credits redeemable for goods at the Chadsey store. This was a win-win arrangement for everyone involved; from the craftsmen who built the 600 looms, to the families who were able to have access to a loom they might never have been able to afford and of course to the Chadsey family. All the while Chadsey and his sons ran the large farm; eventually, upon the return of son Alfred from Massachusetts in 1852, where he was operating a scythe manufacturing plant, changing the focus of that farm from a traditional one to a farm focused solely on seed production. For more on that enterprise see the entry for 140 West Main Street. Towards the end of their days, Jeremiah and Avis Chadsey, both of whom lived into their

90s, sold the house to their nephew and niece Daniel and Eliza Wightman with a life estate allowing them to finish their days there. Jeremiah died in 1873 and Avis in 1874 and both are buried side by side in the Chadsey plot at Elm Grove. Soon after the death of her aunt and uncle, Eliza lost her husband as well and when she eventually remarried to machinist Enos Nickerson, she sold this house and in 1883 moved with him to Providence.

From 1883 until 1899, the house was owned by recent Irish immigrant house carpenter John Mulligan and his wife Ellen. While living here they had four children, John Jr., Charlotte, Mary, and Ann. In 1899, they moved to Narragansett and sold the house to Jonathan T. Nichols who used it in association with the summer hotel "The Elms" which they had created from the circa 1807 double house once shared by Boone and Christopher Spink and their families. When the Elms

The Elms, a summer hotel, was located just west of the Spink house.

burned to the ground in 1905, the Nichols family sold this house to Wickford grocer Michael J. Ryan. Michael Ryan, who at that time lived on Brown Street in the village, purchased this as an investment rental property. He held on to it utilizing it in that way until March of 1926, when he sold it to Robert Bryson.

Robert Bryson was a Scottish born textile industry professional who came to this country to take advantage of opportunities in America's growing textile industry. He was in charge of the dying department of Coventry, RI, textile plant prior to moving to North Kingstown and a career position as the dyeroom foreman at the nearby Hamilton Web narrow weave fabric mill. A devout Catholic he was active at St. Bernards Church. In September of 1941, he sold the house to George C. Cranston Jr.

George Cranston also used the house as an income producing rental property until 1956, when his eldest daughter Gail moved in with her first husband John Allen and daughter Debra on the first floor and his eldest son George Cyrus III moved in on the upper floor with his wife Jean and their first born son, a boy who would one day grow up to obsess about the history of Wickford perhaps a bit too much. Later George Cranston Jr. signed over ownership of the home to Gail and she, to this day, still lives there with her second husband Frederick (Ted) Seymour.

Gail and Ted Seymour have no equal when it comes to living lives of service to their community and the world around them. Ted, a farmer, skilled carpenter and a commercial fisherman began his working career as a Saunderstown dairy farmer who also served a stint as the live-in caretaker at historic Casey Farms. After leaving the life of a dairy farm he began a successful contracting business with his brother focused on new home construction and home renovation, along the way he mentored many the area's most successful home builders today. After a career as a contractor Ted "switched gears" and began a third career as a lobster fisherman. Along the way he somehow found time to be the inspirational driving force and founding member behind, not only South County Habitat for Humanity, but also the Welcome House of South County, the region's premier homeless shelter. He also served the community groups Meals on Wheels and Friends in Service Helping (FISH), an all-volunteer organization that helps those in need. Ted also became an Episcopal lay reader and deacon and was active in more than one Episcopal parish in South County. He was honored with a United Way Jefferson Award for his selfless dedication to aiding his fellow man for these efforts. Gail (Cranston) Seymour is a beloved wife, mother, grandmother (and aunt I might add) who is blessed with remarkable musical abilities and worked for years as an organist in her father's business and in nearby churches. She was the founder and driving force behind Joseph's Coat Thrift-shop, a faith-based used clothing shop ran in partnership for two decades with North Kingstown area churches, and also worked tirelessly for both Meals on Wheels and FISH. She too was trained as an Episcopal lay reader and at the time of her confirmation as such was one of the very first women to serve in that position. Ted and Gail are "retired" now, but of course they actually never stop serving their fellow man; Ted is now an advocate for community gardening in North Kingstown. These two people are extraordinary; it is an honor to be able to call them Aunt Gail and Uncle Ted.

Gail and Ted Seymour

ALFRED B. CHADSEY – 1852

157.   *140 West Main Street*

B ack in 1815, when Alfred Chadsey was born, most farmers in North Kingstown as well as the rest of the U.S. used fertilizers consisting of processed animal products (i.e., fish or bone meal, guano, and manure); they also retained a portion of their crop each year as seed for the next year's sowing. By the time of his death some eighty-seven years later in 1902, these two as well as many other facets of farming had changed drastically and Chadsey, a man trained at the Washington Academy (present day site of Wickford elementary) as a school teacher, had played an important part in the modernization of agriculture in America.

Alfred Chadsey was born into a family deeply rooted in North Kingstown history. The first Chadsey to settle here had come from Wales, via Newport, and settled into a farm on the old section of the Boston Post Road we now know as Chadsey Road as early as 1716. Little did William Chadsey know that someday, the very road he lived upon would be renamed after his illustrious descendant, in honor of his contributions to the very livelihood he was undertaking. Alfred's father, Jeremiah Chadsey was, a number of generations later, carrying on in the family tradition as a farmer, not only there, but also at a different location, just up the hill from Wickford on the south side of the Grand Highway (West Main Street). Jeremiah, however, was a man of ambition and industry; in addition to his farm, he also ran a store in Wickford, as well as a home hand-loom weaving business which at its peak involved 600 families spread out over all of the adjoining communities. In 1835, as his father's enterprises expanded, Alfred resigned from his teaching position at one of the town's district schools and entered into a partnership with him. He struck out on his own in 1844, entering into a partnership with acquaintances, Stephen Draper and John Brown, for the purposes of starting a scythe manufacturing plant in Leicester, Massachusetts. In 1852, homesick for the familiar environs of Wickford, he sold his share to his partners and moved back to North Kingstown where he took over the management of the family farm. This home on West Main Street was constructed on land given to Alfred "with love and affection" at that time. This move was as important for the future of agriculture in the region as it was for Alfred and his family.

Alfred was more than likely aware of the fact that in order to be a success in a rather run-of-the-mill occupation like farming it was important to find a niche in which one could stand head and shoulders above the rest. He decided to make the raising of crops specifically for seed production, not food, his specialty and he entered into this area of expertise with the benefit of his education and scientific background. This was a relatively new way to farm and not without risk. In order to stack the deck in his favor he decided to experiment with another relatively new advance in farming, chemical fertilizers. He had success with them but found them to be too expensive; with that in mind, he set out to concoct this own fertilizer compounds. After some trial and error he was able to produce a chemical fertilizer which was both effective and affordable. As a member of the executive committee of both the state and Washington County Agricultural

Societies, he was able to publish his findings and pass on this success to the agricultural community across the state as well as the region. Back on the farm, Alfred was bringing in record crops of seeds. His onion, beet, carrot, and turnip seeds were harvested by the ton, no small accomplishment if you have ever seen the size of one of these seeds, and sold to wholesalers all over the nation. Chadsey was considered a man of merit in the local community and held many positions of importance; he was a state representative, town council president, and superintendent of schools for North Kingstown. He also sat on the boards of trustees of two banks in town. During the Civil War, Chadsey was the Provost Marshal for RI's second district. Finally, after the war, he was an unsuccessful candidate for Lt. Governor. A devout Baptist, his fer-

Alfred B. Chadsey
From History of Washington and Kent Counties, Rhode Island, 1889, by J. R. Cole.

140 West Main Street prior to the addition on the front.

vent support of prohibition probably cost him the election. In spite of this, at his life's end in February of 1902, Alfred Chadsey was a man who had contributed much to his community, his state, and, most importantly his vocation – farming. Sadly, he is remembered by too few, and only the road which was renamed after him stands in testimony to his outstanding life.

The Chadsey farm on West Main Street in Wickford, extended all the way south to Phillips Street and east to Academy Hill and Cove. His grand home, was sold, by his daughter Ellen (Chadsey) Reynolds in September of 1908 to George C. Cranston Sr., and his been continually occupied by "The Cranston's of Wickford" funeral home since that date.

George C. Cranston Sr.

THE OLD TOWN HOUSE – 1807

158.   **136 West Main Street**

This building was constructed in 1807 by ship and house carpenter William Holloway on a lot of land donated to the Town of North Kingstown by Daniel and James Updike the year previous. Town Treasurer Benjamin Davis ceremonially paid the Updikes with a 5 shilling piece at the annual town meeting in 1806. William Holloway's bent towards ship building can be seen in the construction details of this simple one story assembly hall. After 150 years of

The Town Hall constructed in 1889.

holding monthly or quarterly Town Council meetings in various private homes and taverns across Kingstowne and later North Kingstown, the elected officials of the community finally had a dedicated meeting space in 1807. The business of the Town of North Kingstown was accomplished here from 1807 until construction of the North Kingstown Town Hall on Boston Neck road in 1889.

After 1889, the Town House was utilized as the meeting hall for the CC Baker Chapter of the GAR, which was a fraternal organization for Civil

The Charles C. Baker Post of the Grand Army of the Republic.

The Veterans of Foreign Wars (V.F.W.) outside the Old Town House.

War Veterans, and then as the meeting hall for the Washington County Post #12 of the American Legion, the prevalent veterans organization that was successor to the GAR after the death of the last few remaining Civil War soldiers and the end of WWI. The Old Town House was also utilized as emergency classroom space by the North Kingstown School Department on a few occasions, most notably after the loss by fire of the Wickford Academy building in 1906.

In 1953, the building was declared surplus by the Town of North Kingstown and was purchased by George C. Cranston Jr. and utilized for many years as the casket showroom for the Cranston's of Wickford funeral home. It is still owned and maintained by the Cranston/Murphy Funeral Home to this day.

SECOR/TOWNEND HOUSE – 1929

159.   **130 West Main Street**

This house was constructed in 1929 for George Secor and his second wife Sarah (Townend) Secor. George Secor, who was born in Caxsaukie, New York, came to Wickford with his parents at the age of 10, and was working as a janitor for the North Kingstown School department covering the high school classes. An avid and active member of the Wickford Methodist Episcopal Church, he joined St. Paul's Episcopal Church when the M.E. congregation disbanded. He died in 1936 at the age of 65 and soon after, his widow Sarah sold the house to her adopted brother Jesse Townend.

Sarah (Townend) Secor

Jesse Townend was born James Henry Howard on December 31, 1893 to Joseph and Hannah (Crompton) Howard. Four days after his birth, his mother died due to complications stemming from the childbirth. Eventually, Joseph allowed his sister-in-law and brother-in-law William and Mary (Crompton) Townend to adopt Jesse. In this way Jesse's aunt and uncle became his parents. Jesse worked much of his life in textile mills, beginning at the age of 13 years old when he became a mill boy

Beatrice and Jesse Townend

working at the Gregory Mill in the village making $1.00 per week. He later worked at the Rodman Mill in nearby Lafayette, eventually becoming a loom fixer, leaving the position only upon the mill's closure. He finished his working life at the Belleville Highway garage on Tower Hill Road. Jesse's wife Beatrice (Dore) Townend was a working woman in a timeframe when most stayed home as mothers and housewives. From 1932 until 1942, she was a teacher in the North Kingstown School system, and from 1942 until 1962 she was the principal of the Quonset Elementary School. They lived the remainder of their lives in this home with Beatrice passing on in December of 1976 and Jesse joining her in October of 1984 just shy of his 91st birthday. The house was left to their daughter Grace who lived here until 2002. The house has since been owned by the Donohue family and its present owner, the Byrnes.

Postcard looking west up West Main Street.

DANIEL VERY – 1851

160.   *126 West Main Street*

This house was constructed in 1851 for local house painter Daniel Very on land he purchased in late 1850 from real estate speculator Charles Allen. Daniel Very (who also sometimes spelled his last name as Verry) was born in 1803 in the Quidnessett section of town, the son of farmer Elijah Very. His early years were spent working with his father and brothers on the family farm which was located off of present day Essex Road. But, when he came of age, as he was not the eldest son and would not be inheriting the farm, he was expected to find his own way in the world. He was quite successful in his chosen trade in large part due to the construction boom in North Kingstown associated with the textile industry. In late 1863, Very, who was by then 60 years old, sold the house and moved back to the Very/Verry family farm. Daniel Very died in 1883/4 and is buried in the family graveyard under one of the most enigmatic gravestones in all of Rhode Island. The simple marble stone, which has broken in two over the years, reads, "Here lies a lump of democracy." Equally mysterious is the fact that Daniel Very's death is officially recorded in the Town records as having occurred on Jan. 11, 1883

Daniel Very's epitaph

and Jan. 11, 1884. As the death date is not carved into his gravestone, it is not certain in which year he met his maker.

The next owner of this home was textile manufacturer and entrepreneur Syria Vaughan. Vaughan, at that time, was the owner of the Hamilton Web textile mill and is widely considered to be the father of the narrow weave textile industry. Syria and his wife Louise (Hamilton) lived elsewhere in a fine home and purchased this house initially as an investment property. However, in 1866, the home became an integral part of a house swap/sale through which Syria and Louise Vaughan became owners of the fine Rufus Sweet house just across the street from this home, and Rufus and Mary (Congdon) Sweet moved into this, their retirement home.

Retired master tailor Rufus Sweet and his wife Mary lived out the remainder of their lives here in this house. Eventually, they transferred ownership of the home to their son Daniel Congdon Sweet, one of the village's earliest and most successful insurance agents, as he was taking care of their affairs. Mary passed away in late 1889 and Rufus joined her for all eternity at Elmgrove Cemetery in March of 1890. Daniel sold the house a year later to Mary E. Reynolds.

Daniel C. Sweet

Mary E. Reynolds of New York City owned this house from August of 1891 through July of 1903. As there were in excess of 40 women living in the five boroughs of New York during that timeframe with that name, no specific information beyond the fact that she was unmarried during this period has been identified. She may be a relation to Charles Boyer Reynolds who also came to Wickford from New York during this era, but that too has not been confirmed as of this

Robert Aldrich Sr.   **Robert Aldrich Jr.**   **Robert Aldrich III**

writing. She may also be the unidentified Mary E. Reynolds buried without a gravestone in the Daniel Sweet family plot at Elmgrove Cemetery.

In July of 1903, Mary Reynolds sold the house to another unmarried older woman, Caroline Newton. Caroline, who lived at that time on Main Street in a home she had shared with her sister, evidently purchased this as an investment property and rented it out to provide herself with a monthly income. After her death in 1912, the house was sold by her estate to prominent Providence-based wholesale merchant and grocer Edward Sherman Aldrich.

Aldrich purchased the house for the use of his son Robert, who, in spite of his degree from Brown University obtained in 1903, desired a life focused upon the sea. Robert Aldrich moved here with his wife Elizabeth (Cocroft) and their children and, after purchasing the 52 ft. fishing vessel *Daniel and Carrie* began a life as a lobster fisherman. With his father's wholesale grocery distribution business as a regular client, he was a quite successful lobsterman. Robert Aldrich's career as a fisherman was interrupted by service as a Navy Officer during WWI. Between that War and WWII Aldrich returned to fishing and also worked for a time in local textile mills. During WWII he served again as an officer in both the US Coast Guard and the merchant marine. After the Second World War Aldrich retired; he passed away in December of 1948. He had been active in St. Paul's Church throughout his life and had served on the Town's School Committee. Additionally he was a perennial democratic candidate for elective office but did not get elected beyond his time on the school committee. Upon his death the house passed down to his son Robert Aldrich Jr. and his wife Katherine and their family. Robert Jr. also served in the US Navy and had a long career at Bostich Manufacturing. When he died in 2003, the home was left to his son Robert III, who in turn willed the home to his sister Penny (Aldrich) Geuss at the end of his life. Ninety seven years after Edward Aldrich's purchase of the home, it is still owned by lovingly maintained by an Aldrich family member.

SUPREME COURT JUSTICE
SYLVESTER SHEARMAN – 1854

161.   *110 West Main Street*

This fine Greek-Revival styled home was constructed in 1854 by Sylvester Shearman on land he purchased from the estate of Richard Boone Eldred. At the time of its purchase, the lot included "the old dwelling house of Robert Eldred," which Shearman must have demolished when he had this house constructed. Sylvester Shearman was North Kingstown born and educated and had studied the law under Wilkins Updike and John Hall. He practiced law here for a time and also in 1842 was elected to the RI General Assembly. In 1848 he was chosen as RI Speaker of the House, the most powerful position in all of State government, he held that post until 1854, at which time he was appointed to the RI Supreme Court. The demands of that position motivated him to purchase a home in Providence, but he also, at the same time, had this home built to serve as his primary home when court was in recess. Shearman lived here with his wife Priscilla (Arnold) and their sons Sumner and William. Both of these young men received Divinity degrees from Brown University and went on to be ordained as Episcopal priests. Additionally the elder son, Sumner, served with honor during the Civil War rising to the rank of Captain. Capt. Sumner Shearman involved in action at Antietam, Fredericksburg, and the Crater, was captured by the Confederacy and was held for six months in a POW camp in Columbia South Carolina. Fearing for his son's life, Judge Shearman eventually had to use his influence to arrange for a POW exchange that included Sumner. Rev. Sumner served the Episcopal community in Jamaica Plain and Rev. William served in Providence, New York state, and then California. Judge Sylvester Shearman, who died in 1868 and was remembered as a principled jurist "without any pretence to superior sanctity," sold this house in 1865 after both of his sons and their families left the state. It was purchased by Walter Waterman.

Providence native Walter Waterman was born Walter Waterman Gudgeon. His birth occurred in 1814; and by 1821, his life took a turn for the worse when his father John Gudgeon died suddenly leaving his wife Sarah (Wilbur) to raise a family on her own. Four years later, Walter's older brother John Jr. died as well. Things were not going well in the Gudgeon family. At some point after that, Walter, who was a whiz on horseback, took that leap of faith and ran off to join the circus. He next shows up in the historic record with a new name of sorts; Walter W. Gudgeon is now Walter Waterman, expert equestrian with the Mabie's Circus, a travelling troupe, one of hundreds crisscrossing the nation in the middle 1800s, formed by Jeremiah and Edmond Mabie who were originally from Patterson NY. The Mabie Circus travelled the nation through Spring, Summer, and early Fall and then hunkered down each winter on the big Mabie-owned 400 acre spread, a former farm, in Delavan, Wisconsin. Between 1847 and 1894, Delavan was home to 26 circus companies. The Mabie Brothers U.S. Olympic Circus, then the largest in America, arrived in 1847, to become the first circus to quarter in the territory of Wisconsin. Its famous rogue elephant, "Romeo," stood 19½ feet high and weighed 10,500 pounds. The original P.T. Barnum Circus was organized here by William C. Coup and Dan Costello. Walter Waterman was a part of all this. After the Mabie boys retired in 1856, Walter went off with the Buckley's National Circus and served as their "Equestrian Director and Ring Master."

After a few years with Buckley's, Walter hit the big time when he took the same position with the P. T. Barnum Show. Walter Waterman was now a star; the poor boy from Rhode Island was at the pinnacle of his game – in the center ring each night for P. T. Barnum.

Walter, though, never forgot his roots, in 1865 he purchased a fine house on West Main Street in Wickford of all places, where he could "winter over" each year. He moved his elderly mother Sarah Gudgeon in and had his sister Anna and her husband Addison Fairbanks and their two daughters Ardelia and Helen move in as well to take care of the day-to-day business of running the place. I can only imagine how proud Sarah must have felt regarding her son the circus star. That's the way things went on for years. Walter would be around each winter and be off the rest of the year travelling the nation as P. T. Barnum's Ringmaster and Equestrian director. The Fairbanks family would hold "down the fort" here in Wickford, with Ardelia's son Addison Luther eventually becoming the Town's very first Librarian and her sister Helen marrying local lad James R. S. Wightman. Anna Gudgeon died here in Wickford and was buried back up in Providence. And one day in October of 1880, the Fairbanks clan in Wickford received a sad telegram from the P. T. Barnum Travelling Circus. Walter Waterman died suddenly while the show was performing in Little Rock, Arkansas. The Circus paid for his funeral and grave plot in Little Rock and that was that – "The Show Must Go On!" and it did. I have not discovered if the Gudgeon/Fairbanks clan ever got a chance to go out and visit his grave. Addison and Anna Fairbanks purchased the house from Walter's estate.

Addison Fairbanks was a retired steamboat mechanic who had worked for the NY Line steamships in their Stonington, Connecticut, repair shop. They lived here with their daughter Ardelia who had divorced her husband, steam engineer Hezekiah Luther, in 1866, and her son Addison. Ardelia worked as a dressmaker with a shop in Wickford until 1890, and Addison was the well known and popular first ever librarian for the town of North Kingstown and the organist for both St. Paul's Church in Wickford and the St. Gabriel's Episcopal Mission Church in nearby Lafayette. Upon Addison Fairbanks death in 1896, the house was left to Ardelia and upon her death in 1917 it became Addison Luther's. In 1918, Addison Luther sold the house to Frank and Sarah Follansbee, with the included caveat that he would be allowed to board here at a reduced rate for the remainder of his life. Addison Luther died in May of 1921.

In 1918, the Reverend Frank J. Follansbee was beginning his second term of service as the pastor of the Wickford Methodist Episcopal Church. He first served the West Main Street congregation in 1877 and later served in Providence, New Bedford, Portsmouth, and Hull, Massachusetts. Prior to becoming a Methodist Episcopal priest, Follansbee served in the US Army and spent five years fighting out west in the Indian Wars under General William "Pecos Bill" Shafter. While in the service he met his wife Sarah (Potts) in Sheridan Wyoming. Sadly, just a year after accepting the position of pastor here in Wickford, Follansbee became ill and died a year later after a long and arduous illness. His wife Sarah stayed on in Wickford after his death and supported herself by taking in boarders. In 1922 she sold her home to Sadie Woodmansee.

Unfortunately, little can be learned about Sadie Woodmansee and her husband Ernest, who was a master mechanic and shop foreman at Brown & Sharpe in Providence. Census records consistently show that they lived in a home in Cranston, where Sadie also worked as a milliner, and they may have either used this home as a country retreat or as strictly an investment rental property. Sadie owned the house from 1922 until she sold it in 1944 to Julius Barske.

Julius Barske came to North Kingstown from his native Connecticut to work as a mechanics foreman at Quonset Naval Air Station, a career he continued until retirement. He was also active locally in the Masons and raised a family here in this house. Julius died in 1966 and his family held on to this house until 1979, when they sold it to its present owners Mike and Patricia Suvari, who are ironically enough a municipal judge and a librarian.

FRANK W. SHERMAN BUTCHERSHOP – 1913

162.   **100 West Main Street**

This building, originally a commercial structure, was constructed in 1913 by butcher and former Belleville grocery store owner Frank Sherman, who had moved here to Wickford, with his wife Effie (Stone) and two children Effie and Howard, from nearby Belleville and purchased the house immediately to the east at 96 West Main St. Sherman had operated a full scale grocery store while in Belleville, but here in Wickford he scaled back his operation and opened up a full service butchershop from which he also ran a butcher's cart which traveled through the nearby villages, offering not only freshly butchered meat for sale, but also the services that a butcher could provide in an era when folks still raised livestock at their homes for eventual consumption by their family. Additionally, in a time before large scale refrigeration and freezing was commonplace, butchers such as Frank Sherman were skilled in the arts of smoking and brining various meat products in order to preserve them for longer periods of time. Frank Sherman finally retired for good, after 50 years of wielding a butcher's knife, in 1931.

A while after closing his butcher shop, Sherman remodeled the building and rented it out to photographer Charles Kendall who opened a photography studio here aided by his wife Frances. The Kendalls did portrait photography here in the building and also went out into the community, photographing everything from weddings to Christmas parties to fabric mill company picnics and employee group photographs. Numerous professionally shot photos from the 1930s and

40s can be identified as Kendall Studio photos by the identifying stamp found on the back of the image. One of the textile mill owners that Kendall worked for was Hamilton Web's owner Joseph W. Greene. When Greene purchased 96 West Main St. from Effie Rulison, Frank Sherman's daughter, he became the Kendall's landlord as well, as this building was part of 96 West Main's property. Kendall Photography stayed here until 1948, and after it closed up shop, Joseph Greene made dramatic changes to the old butchershop building.

The first thing Joseph Greene did was move the building, which had always been located on the sidewalk just as 96 West Main is today, back onto a new foundation installed immediately behind it. He then reconfigured the building's facade from a look that was decidedly late 19th

century commercial to one that was late 18th century residential.

Joseph Warren Greene Sr.

To convincingly pull this off, Greene purchased the front door and two windows from the circa 1757 sexton's cottage of the Wickford Baptist Church which was being demolished in April of that year and had them installed in this building. He then had the interior of the building remodeled into a small residential cottage. This cottage, along with the larger home at 96 West Main is still owned by a descendant of Joseph W. Greene.

The old Sexton's cottage

A sign for Kendall's Studio hangs outside the former butchershop.

SAMUEL DYER – 1813

163.   **96 West Main Street**

This house was built for Samuel and Lydia Dyer on a lot he purchased in 1812 from George Nichols. Little information can be found regarding the Dyers; he called himself a yeoman on all legal documents, this would indicate that he was a farmer and probably farmed acreage located elsewhere while living here in the village. This was a common practice at the time and runs contrary to the later tradition in which a family lives right on the property that they farmed. In 1816, Dyer sold the house to retired farmer Sylvester Pearce. Pearce lived here until 1821 when he sold it to local attorney John Hall.

As the century turned, and the 1800s began, most small New England communities had but a handful each of truly educated citizens. Beyond the major cities, folks who could "read, write, and cipher" were few and far between in an age long before public schooling was instituted. Don't get me wrong, there was no shortage of highly intelligent and competent people at that time, it's just that book learning was largely a luxury reserved for the affluent minority. In North Kingstown, Attorney John Hall was one of those highly educated folks. If you wanted a real estate or business transaction done 'right and proper' it was to John Hall that you turned. Need an important letter written for you, or read to you for that matter – John Hall was your guy. Trouble with a neighbor; John Hall will take care of that for you. You want a well written character reference or letter of introduction? Again John Hall was your man.

John Hall was born in 1780, the eldest of the eleven children of Slocum and Almy (Fry) Hall, in the Hall Homestead on the Boston Post Road. His birthplace, constructed in 1676, still exists to this day as the Hall-Northup House near the RI State Police barracks and is one of New England's oldest private homes. After completing his education and legal training and then marrying Patience Peckham, the daughter of Benedict and Mary (Eldred) Peckham, he purchased a fine home on the Grand Highway into Wickford (now West Main Street) and set up shop as a lawyer; one of two in North Kingstown, the other being the equally learned Wilkins Updike. John Hall, along with Updike and others, was also instrumental in the founding of the Washington Academy in Wickford, a true institution of higher learning and a place where it is thought that he taught as well. Additionally, John and Patience Hall raised four children, sons Louriston and John and daughters Amanda and Harriet.

Politically, John Hall was a member of a small but fervent movement in the early 1800s, the Anti-Masonic Party. The thrust of this movement is self evident and it was populated by many prominent Quakers like John Hall, as well as numerous others, including well known Bostonian and future President John Quincy Adams, a man with whom Hall became acquainted through this party. Hall and Adams corresponded on occasion and in February of 1837, Hall used this connection to pass a petition on to Washington DC, signed by the women of Wickford village promoting the cause of the Abolition of Slavery in the District of Columbia.

John Hall died suddenly at an Anti-Mason Convention in Providence on February 18, 1846. According to his friend and fellow Wickfordite John Jonathan Reynolds, he passed away suddenly after dinner while sitting and enjoying a cigar and good conversation with friends. In mid-sentence "they saw in death his eyelids close, calmly as to a night's repose." He was buried in the Hall graveyard just behind the place of his birth with noted Quaker Thomas Anthony performing the funeral service. Sadly, after his death, the disposition of his house and office in Wickford was embroiled in a long legal battle, as he left it to his young nephew Christopher Tillinghast in his will and Tillinghast had perished around the same time. The Halls and Tillinghasts battled over ownership of the house for quite some time until North Kingstown's other learned man, Wilkins Updike, negotiated a fair settlement between the powerful and connected Tillinghasts of East Greenwich and the equally well connected Halls of North Kingstown. This agreement, which was eventually brought before the RI General Assembly by Updike for final approval, mandated the sale of the house and an equal final disposition of the funds realized by the sale. This took until October of 1848 when the home was finally sold to local grocer Isaac C. Champlin.

Isaac Champlin, who was married to John and Patience Hall's niece, Ann Peckham, ran a grocery store in the village, located where the Gregory Building now stands, for many years. They initially shared the home, which they made into a two family, with their adult son Benedict Peckham Champlin, who worked in the locket factory in Wickford, and his wife Jane (Washburn) and their four children. After Benedict and his family moved to Providence after the locket factory closed, they rented that space to local seamstresses Ann Davis and Deborah Gardiner and Ann's sister Lucy Davis who was a school teacher. Isaac died in 1862 and his widow stayed in the home until 1866 when she sold it to James A. Greene.

James A. Greene was born in Warwick, RI, and traced his ancestry back to General Nathanael Greene and beyond. Prior to 1866 he worked with his father Joseph and his Pittman relations as a jeweler and silversmith in New York City. He came back to Rhode Island with his wife Sarah (Cutler) Greene and became a partner with Syria Vaughan in the Hamilton Web narrow weave textile company. He served initially as the mill's treasurer and later, after Vaughan sold his interests in the company, became its sole owner. James Greene held on to this house for only a short while; desirous of a home with a lot large enough to expand upon, in 1870 he swapped houses with his neighbor to the immediate east, Capt. Vincent Gardiner.

For Capt. Vincent Gardiner, a lifelong mariner, this was a retirement home for only a short while. He died in April of 1872 and his wife Mary, daughter of prominent local businessman and East Indies trader Jonathan Reynolds, stayed in the house living for a time with her adult son Leander Gardiner. After Leander, who suffered with epilepsy, died at the age of 37, her son Capt. Jonathan Vincent Gardiner and his wife Charlotte moved in to the house. In an interesting coincidence Charlotte, daughter of Slocum and Charlotte Hall was also a niece to John Hall. Mary Gardiner died in 1901 at the age of 94. Jonathan and Charlotte stayed in the house until 1913 and then sold it to Frank W. Sherman.

Frank Sherman moved into the house with his wife Effie (Stone) and two children Howard and Effie. A butcher by trade, for many years, he operated a grocery and meat market in the busy mill village of Belleville and had moved here to Wickford with the idea of downsizing this operation a bit. He had a butcher shop built on the property right next door (see 100 West Main St. for details) and ran a meat cart out of here as well. Frank lost his wife Effie in 1919 and eventually married again to Celia Eaton. After his children left the house, he rented rooms to two widows, Phebe (Phillips) Rathbun, widow of Lauriston Rathbun and a relation Abbie Sherman. Frank Sherman retired from the butcher's life in 1931 and sadly perished in 1934 due to injuries he sustained when falling off the roof of the large shed on the property. His daughter Effie

Rulison held on to the property until 1944, renting the house and the former butcher shop building to photographer Charles Kendall. In 1944 she sold it to Joseph Warren Greene, the son of former owner James A. Greene, who now lived next door. Since 1944 the house been owned by descendants of Joseph Warren Greene and has been occupied by various Greene relations and/or tenants.

Captain Vincent Gardiner Jr. — 1833/1871

164.   *90 West Main Street*

The front peak-roofed portion of this complex two-story, cross gabled house with a three story mansard roofed addition with its dramatic tower on the eastern end, was constructed in 1833 for Packetmaster Vincent Gardiner Jr. and his wife Mary (Reynolds) by Wickford house carpenter Benoni Bates. Gardiner had been given the lot earlier that year by his father Vincent Sr. and Uncle David Gardiner. This parcel of land, at one time, had been the location of a Holloway family owned shipyard where vessel hulls were constructed. Those hulls were launched here in Academy Cove and then, after the decking of the old Elamsville Bridge was temporarily removed, were floated to other yards for finishing out. The Gardiner brothers had purchased the parcel from the Tillinghast family who had in turn acquired it from the Holloways. Construction of this house was financed in part by Mary M. Gardiner's father, wealthy merchant and East Indies trader Jonathan Reynolds. Vincent expanded the parcel in 1855, when he purchased the undeveloped house lot to the immediate west from Othneil Brown, who had by then relocated to Genesee County, New York.

Mary M. Gardiner
From *Souvenir History of the New England Southern Conference*

Capt. Vincent Gardiner was the master of the Providence packet boats *Lucy Emeline* and *Eagle* on their daily runs from Wickford to the capital city throughout most of the middle portion of the 19th century. He was also a part owner, along with his uncle David, of numerous other sailing vessels, including *Fox, Accomodater, Helen, Temperance,* and *General Battey* during that same timeframe. Vincent and Mary raised a number of children in this home, including daughters Mary Eleanor, who married Rev. C. H. Payne of the Wickford Methodist Episcopal Church, Susan who married Thomas Nichols, and sons Leander and Capt. Jonathan Vincent Gardiner who married Charlotte Hall. In September of 1870, as part of a house swap, the Gardiners moved next door into the house at 96 West Main Street and James A. Greene and his family assumed ownership of this home.

By 1870, James A. Greene was the sole owner of the very successful Hamilton Web textile mill in the nearby village of Hamilton. He arranged this house swap with the Gardiners because he was desirous of a larger parcel of land upon which he might construct a family home worthy of his station in life. He incorporated the 1833 home into the design of his new house which was grand on the scale expected for a successful mill owner of the time. The attached tower, although definitely an attractive architectural addition to the building, was practical and functional in nature in that its attic contains a large oaken tank which was utilized to operate indoor plumbing; so that, like the nearby Rodmans of Lafayette, no wife or daughter of James Greene would ever have to use an outhouse again. For many decades, a windmill on the property was utilized to pump water to keep the tank full. Support beams still seen in the basement of the 1871 mansard roofed addition to the house consist of sections of ship's masts which were doubtlessly still found on the property harkening back to its time as a shipyard site. James Greene and his wife Sarah lived out their lives in this house with Sarah passing on in 1902 and James in 1921. The house was left to their son Joseph Warren Greene who also had assumed control of Hamilton Web. To this day, it still remains in the ownership of a direct descendant of James Greene, making it, with 142 years and counting, the home in the village held by one family for the longest period of time. Its present owner Joseph Beckwith, maintains it in a manner that would be infinitely pleasing to his great great grandfather James Anthony Greene.

James Anthony Greene

The Hamilton Web Textile Mill, in the village of Hamilton, was owned by James Anthony Greene and later his son Joseph Warren Greene.

Hamilton Web Co.'s office staff and overseers from *Textile Age Magazine*, October 1944. Front row: (left to right) Harry Taylor, Cecelia T. Power, Joseph Warren Greene Jr., Herbert N. Macdonald, Gladys E. B. Dawley, Fred W. Horsfall. Back row: James Russell, Alfred J. Jecoy, Frederick E. Matteson, Merton J. Wilmarth, Lester P. Burgess.

SUPPORT

The publication of this book would not have been possible without the financial contributions of the following organizations and individuals:

The North Kingstown Arts Council

Historic Wickford Inc.

Mike & Ellen Dacey

Michael & Nancy Donohue

Roberta Grundy

Stephen and Maureen Tyson

Centerville Bank

Daniel & Mimi Dyer

Quonset Auto Body Inc.

Cranston-Murphy Funeral Home

Neil Dunay

Darrell McIntire

Gordon & Kelly Kilday

Dr. Edward Hart DMD

Robert A. Cioe

Pearce, Sylvester 110
Peckham, Benedict 22, 111
Peckham, Benjamin 22
Peckham, Benoni 22
Peckham, Frank 38
Peckham, Frank A. 36
Peckham, Gertrude 38
Peckham, Harold 38
Peckham, Marion 38
Peckham, Mary (nee Eldred) 111
Peckham, Mary (nee Lawton) 22
Peckham, Sarah (nee Hazard) 22
Peckham, Sarah (nee McNamara) 36
Peckham, Thomas Hazard 23
Peckham, Timothy Jr. 23
Peckham, Timothy Russell 22
Peet Family 67
Peirce, Harriet (nee Sunderland) 53
Peirce, John B. 9
Peirce, Samuel W. 78
Peirce, Thomas 9
Peirce, Thomas J. 53
Peirce, Thomas W. 53, 55
Perot, Ross 76
Phelan, Dr. John R. M. 59
Pierce, Charles C. 82
Pierce, Charles C. Jr. 82
Pierce, Hattie A. 82
Pitts, John 26
Pollock, Arthur L. 20
Porter, Helen (nee Talbot) 70
Porter, Helen Talbot 75
Porter, J. Benton 70
Potter Family 51
Pratt, Carl 10
Pratt, Edward 7
Pratt, Mr. 11

Q
Quinn Family 71

R
Randall, Craig 76
Randall Family 79
Rathbun, Baldwin 45
Rathbun, Elizabeth 45
Rathbun, Emeline (nee Tourgee) 45
Rathbun, Jedediah L. 45
Rathbun, Lauriston 112
Rathbun, Phebe (nee Phillips) 112
Rathbun, Philander 45
Rathbun, Philena 45
Reis Family 56
Reis, Francis Sr. 56
Reynolds, Abigail (nee Updike) 39, 45
Reynolds, Benjamin 26, 28
Reynolds, Charles Boyer 103
Reynolds, Elizabeth 28
Reynolds, Elizabeth (nee Gardiner) 29
Reynolds, Ellen (nee Chadsey) 97
Reynolds, George B. 32
Reynolds, Hattie 7
Reynolds, H. Irving 67
Reynolds, Horatio Nelson 32
Reynolds, Isaac 28
Reynolds, Isaac Jr. 29
Reynolds, John Jonathan 111
Reynolds, Jonathan 26, 112, 113
Reynolds, Joseph 39
Reynolds, Joseph G. 5
Reynolds, Mary 32
Reynolds, Mary E. 103
Reynolds, Sheffield 26
Reynolds, Stephen 29
Richmond Family 51
Rodman, Colonel Robert 9
Rodman, Jessie (nee Maglone) 21
Rodman, Mrs. 9
Rodman, Roger 11
Rodman, Roger W. 20

Roessigier, Leigh (nee Hibbard) 51
Roessigier, Peter 51
Romano, Mrs. 9
Roosevelt 73
Rose, Benjamin 78
Rose, John Browning 79
Rose, Rufus 78
Rose, Susan 78
Rose, Susan C. (nee Northup) 78
Rose, William 78
Ross, Frances "Frankie" 53
Rulison, Effie (nee Sherman) 109, 112
Russo, John 79
Ryan, Edward 7
Ryan, Michael J. 93

S
Sabo, Peter 85
Sanford, Esbon 35
Sanford, Esther (nee Chappell) 35
Saunders, Allie 5
Sawyer, Gene 59
Sealey, Joe 11
Secor, George 100
Secor, Sarah (nee Townend) 100
Seymour, Frederick (Ted) 94
Seymour, Gail (Cranston) Allen 94
Shafter, General William "Pecos Bill" 107
Shearman, Priscilla (nee Arnold) 105
Shearman, Sumner 105
Shearman, Sylvester 105
Shearman, William 105
Sherman, Abbie 112
Sherman, Alfred A. 72
Sherman Brothers 29
Sherman, Celia (nee Eaton) 112
Sherman, Effie 108, 112
Sherman, Effie (nee Stone) 108, 112
Sherman, Frank 108
Sherman, Frank W. 112
Sherman, Howard 108, 112
Sherman, Lorena (nee Congdon) 72
Shippee, Alphonso 53, 55
Shippee, Charles 53
Shippee, Harry 30
Shippee, Horace J. 23
Shippee, Lodowick 30
Shippee, Susan 53
Signor, Clarence 71
Signor, Zella 71
Slocum, Jonathan 70, 74
Slocum, Susan 74
Smith, Captain Frank 7
Smith, Joseph 11
Spencer, Henry B. 47
Spink, Anna (nee Boone) 68
Spink, Barbara (nee Lindley) 91
Spink, Boone 31, 77, 91, 93
Spink, Charlotte 91
Spink, Christopher 31, 77, 91, 93
Spink, Daniel 91
Spink, Eugene 78
Spink Family 89
Spink, Hannah 77, 91
Spink, Hannah (nee Boone) 77, 91
Spink, Isaac 78
Spink, Isaac Jr. 78
Spink, Nicholas 68, 77, 91
Spink, Oliver 16
Spink, Samuel 77, 91
Spink, Samuel Jr. 91
Spink, Samuel "Wooden Leg Sammy" 78
Spink, Sarah Ann 91
Spink, Thomas L. 91
Squillante, Christopher 71, 76
Stadig, Charlotte (nee St. Germain) 73
Stadig, Winston Jr. 73
Stadig, Winston W. Sr. 73
Stalin 73
Stearns, Francis 74

Made in the USA
Charleston, SC
16 November 2012